RETIREMENT COLLECTION
FOR WOMEN

2 BOOKS FOR WOMEN READY TO GROW
BEYOND WORK AND LIVE WITH PURPOSE
AND CONFIDENCE TO ENJOY THEIR MOST
REWARDING YEARS

VICTORIA SPRING

TABLE OF CONTENTS

RETIREMENT REDEFINED FOR WOMEN

RETIREMENT BEYOND FINANCES

RETIREMENT REDEFINED FOR WOMEN

NAVIGATE LIFE AFTER WORK WITH CONFIDENCE, BUILD COMMUNITY, EXPLORE PASSIONS, AND STAY ENGAGED TO LIVE YOUR BEST LIFE

VICTORIA SPRING

INTRODUCTION

As I sat across from my dear friend Sarah, watching her eyes brim with tears, I couldn't help but feel a deep sense of empathy. "I thought retirement would be a time of freedom and joy," she confessed, "but instead, I feel lost and alone." Her words echoed the sentiments of countless women I've encountered over the years, each grappling with the profound changes that come with leaving their careers behind.

The unique challenges women face as they transition into retirement have been overlooked for far too long. We're expected to embrace this new chapter gracefully, yet few resources exist to guide us through the complex emotional, social, and financial landscape that lies ahead. It's time to change that narrative.

This book was born from a desire to empower women like Sarah – and like you – to redefine retirement on your own terms. As someone who has walked this path myself, I understand the fears, doubts, and aspirations that come with this significant life shift. My goal is to provide a roadmap that addresses the practical

aspects of retirement planning and delves into the deeper questions of identity, purpose, and fulfillment.

Throughout these pages, we'll explore the holistic dimensions of retirement, from building a solid financial foundation to nurturing meaningful relationships and discovering new passions. You'll find real-life stories from women who have successfully navigated this journey, as well as practical exercises and reflections designed to help you clarify your vision for the future.

But this book is more than a guide; it's an invitation to undertake a transformative journey of self-discovery. As you read, I encourage you to approach each chapter with an open mind and willingness to challenge long-held beliefs about what retirement "should" look like. This is your opportunity to create a life that truly resonates with your values, desires, and dreams.

Together, we'll delve into the art of crafting a retirement that is uniquely yours. We'll explore how to cultivate resilience in the face of change, build a supportive network of like-minded women, and prioritize self-care as you adjust to your new normal. You'll learn strategies for staying mentally sharp, physically active, and emotionally grounded, ensuring your retirement years are filled with vitality and purpose.

As we move through each chapter, you'll gain clarity, confidence, and a renewed sense of excitement for the possibilities that lie ahead. Whether you're on the cusp of retirement or have already taken the leap, this book will serve as a trusted companion, offering guidance, inspiration, and a reminder that you are not alone on this journey.

So, dear reader, I invite you to turn the page and join me on this transformative adventure. Together, we'll redefine retirement and unlock the secrets to crafting a joyful, engaged lifestyle that honors your unique gifts and aspirations. Let's embark on this journey with open hearts and minds, ready to embrace the incredible opportunities that await us in this new chapter of life.

REDEFINING YOUR IDENTITY BEYOND THE CAREER

A t a recent gathering, I met Diane, a woman who, after decades of dedication to her career, stood at the precipice of retirement. "I spent my life defining myself by my work," she shared, "and now, I wonder who I am without my job title." Her words resonate with many women who face similar crossroads. This chapter invites you to explore the exciting opportunity that retirement offers to redefine your identity, not as a loss but as a chance to focus on personal growth, new interests, and uncharted paths. This transition isn't just about retiring from work; it's about rediscovering yourself and embracing a phase rich with potential.

1.1 EMBRACING THE NEW YOU: A PERSONAL JOURNEY

The transition from a career-driven life to one centered on personal identity can feel daunting, yet it holds the promise of transformation. Instead of viewing retirement as an end, see it as a beginning—a time to shift focus from professional roles to personal growth. Reflecting on past achievements and future aspirations can provide clarity. Consider dedicating time to exercises that help you recognize the skills and strengths you've developed over the years. Write them down, celebrate them, and then envision how these can be applied to new pursuits. Reflect on what you've always wanted to explore but never had the time for. This is the moment to let those dreams flourish. To illustrate this, let's look at Catherine Kilty, a nonprofit director who transitioned to a post-retirement life filled with alternative income sources that aligned with her passions. Catherine's story exemplifies how embracing change can lead to a fulfilling and purpose-driven life.

As you embark on this personal journey, it's crucial to foster self-acceptance and growth. This involves acknowledging the emotional aspects of redefining yourself and overcoming the fear of change. Many women find it challenging to move beyond the roles they've held for so long, but developing a growth mindset can ease this transition. Techniques such as cognitive reframing can be invaluable, where you consciously shift negative thoughts to positive ones. Embrace the idea that retirement is a time for reinvention, not regression. By gradually letting go of past job titles and the identity tied to them, you can open the door to new opportunities. Writing a farewell letter to your career can serve as a powerful ritual for closure. Express gratitude for experiences and lessons learned, then consciously release them, making space for the future.

Creating a vision for what lies ahead is a pivotal step in this process. Picture a future where you are free to explore new interests without the constraints of a work schedule. Consider attending a vision board workshop where you can visually map out goals and aspirations. This creative exercise allows you to focus on what truly matters to you and serves as a tangible reminder of your intentions. Goal-setting exercises can also help you chart a course for personal development. Break down your aspirations into steps and set realistic timelines to keep yourself accountable. As you progress, celebrate each milestone, no matter how small, to maintain momentum and motivation.

Reflection Exercise: Mapping Your Past and Future

Take a moment to reflect on your career and personal life. Write down three significant achievements you're proud of and consider how they have shaped you. Then, list three aspirations you have for the future. Reflect on how these aspirations align with your values and passions. How can you begin to integrate these into your daily life? This exercise bridges who you've been and who you're becoming, helping you embrace the new you with confidence.

The journey to redefine your identity beyond your career is as unique as you are. It requires courage and a willingness to embrace change. You can navigate this transition with enthusiasm by focusing on personal growth, recognizing your strengths, and setting new goals. Retirement is not just a phase of life; it's a canvas upon which you can paint a vibrant and fulfilling future. As you continue through this book, let these insights inspire you to explore all this new chapter offers.

1.2 FROM JOB TITLE TO PERSONAL FULFILLMENT

During retirement, a profound shift occurs as we transition our focus from professional achievements to personal satisfaction. This change invites us to redefine fulfillment, moving away from the metrics of job titles and salary increases and toward the more enriching realm of personal values and happiness. Identifying what truly matters to us becomes a guiding compass in this transition. Take a moment to reflect on your core values—those deep-seated beliefs that have shaped your life decisions. Aligning these values with new activities can create a more satisfying and meaningful existence. Whether it's nurturing creativity through painting or fostering connections by volunteering, these pursuits can bring a sense of accomplishment that transcends any corporate accolade.

Finding fulfillment in new roles often means stepping into spaces that resonate with our passions and interests. Volunteering offers a structured way to engage with causes that matter to you, providing a platform to apply your skills and experience in meaningful ways. Consider causes that have tugged at your heartstrings —whether it's mentoring young women entering the workforce or supporting environmental initiatives. These roles can offer personal fulfillment and a chance to contribute positively to society. Community engagement activities further expand this horizon, allowing you to connect with others who share similar interests. Join local clubs or groups focused on gardening, book discussions, or any activity that sparks joy. Engaging with your community in this way enriches your life and builds a network of support and camaraderie.

As we redefine success, shifting our perspective from achieving external accolades to cultivating internal happiness and fulfillment becomes essential. Success is no longer measured by promotions or bonuses but by the joy and satisfaction that come from living authentically. Create new metrics for personal success that reflect your current priorities, such as the quality of your relationships, the depth of your experiences, or your impact on your community. Exploring unconventional success stories can provide inspiration. Consider the story of a woman who became an accomplished writer in her retirement years, using her life experiences as rich material for her novels. Her success wasn't defined by traditional standards but by the fulfillment she found in expressing herself through storytelling.

Interactive Exercise: Defining Your Personal Fulfillment

Take a few moments to jot down what personal fulfillment means to you. List activities or roles that align with your core values and bring you joy. Reflect on how these pursuits might redefine success in your life. Consider how they contribute to your sense of purpose and happiness. Use this exercise as a foundation for exploring new opportunities that resonate with your true self.

The exploration of new possibilities is an exciting aspect of this phase. Retirement offers the freedom to try activities you may have never considered before. Attend workshops or classes on novel subjects that pique your curiosity, whether learning a new language, exploring culinary arts, or diving into digital photography. These experiences provide intellectual stimulation and open doors to new friendships and interests. The key is to approach each opportunity with an open mind and a willingness to embrace the unknown. As you engage with these new activities, you'll find that personal fulfillment is not a destination but a continual process of growth and discovery.

This shift from job titles to personal fulfillment is a transformative process that invites you to explore deeper aspects of yourself. It's about embracing the freedom to pursue what truly matters and finding joy in the everyday moments. As you navigate this transition, remember that personal fulfillment is an ongoing journey that evolves as you do. It's a path where every experience adds richness to your life, painting a picture of success defined by happiness and contentment.

1.3 WRITING YOUR NEXT CHAPTER: PERSONAL DEVELOPMENT PLANS

As you stand on the threshold of retirement, consider the possibilities that lie ahead. This time in your life provides the perfect opportunity to craft a personal development plan—a structured approach to growth that acknowledges your past while embracing your future. Such planning isn't about filling time; it's about enriching your life with purpose and intention. The first step is to outline a clear vision of what you wish to achieve, both in the short and long term. Begin by identifying areas where you want to grow, whether it's learning a new language, mastering a musical instrument, or enhancing your physical fitness. By setting specific, measurable goals, you create a roadmap that guides you toward meaningful accomplishments.

Creating a personal development plan involves more than just listing aspirations. It requires a thoughtful process of goal setting and reflection. Use an outline to break down your goals into actionable steps. This approach clarifies your objectives and makes them feel attainable. For instance, if your goal is to learn French, start with a short-term goal of completing an introductory course. Then, set a long-term goal of traveling to France to practice your skills. Breaking down these goals into smaller, manageable tasks helps maintain focus and motivation. With each step, you build confidence and move closer to realizing your ambitions.

Tracking your progress is essential to personal development. Regularly monitoring your achievements allows you to celebrate successes and identify areas for improvement. Journaling can be an effective tool for self-reflection, offering insights into your journey and helping you adjust your plans as needed. Document your thoughts, challenges, triumphs, and use this record to gain perspective on your growth. Additionally, consider using apps designed for goal tracking. These tools provide reminders, track milestones, and offer a visual representation of your progress, keeping you motivated.

A commitment to lifelong learning is essential for personal development. Engaging in continuing education enhances cognitive function and provides a sense of purpose. This stage of life presents the ideal opportunity to dive into subjects that spark your interest. Whether you enroll in online courses or attend local classes, the wealth of knowledge available is vast and varied. Learning something new, such as playing the piano or taking a cooking class, stimulates the mind and enriches your daily life. This pursuit of knowledge ensures that you remain curious, engaged, and intellectually active.

When setting goals, it's crucial to remain realistic and achievable. The SMART framework—specific, measurable, attainable, relevant, and time-bound—offers a practical method for structuring your objectives. By defining clear parameters, you create a focused path to success. This method encourages setting attainable goals that align with your capabilities and resources. Celebrate your progress along the way, acknowledging each milestone as a victory. These small successes fuel motivation and provide the encouragement needed to pursue larger goals.

1.4 PERSONAL DEVELOPMENT TEMPLATE: SETTING GOALS

Consider using a personal development guide to structure your goals. Start by writing down your long-term aspirations and breaking them into short-term objectives. For each goal, list the specific steps required to achieve it and set a timeline for completion. This guide serves as a map of your journey, keeping you organized and focused. Regularly review and adjust your plan to ensure it remains aligned with your evolving interests and priorities.

Personal development is a lifelong endeavor, one that evolves as you do. By actively pursuing growth, you create a rich and fulfilling retirement experience. This chapter in your life offers the freedom to explore new interests, deepen your knowledge, and cultivate skills that enrich your existence. As you embrace this process, remember that personal development is not about reaching an endpoint but about enjoying the journey of self-discovery and transformation.

1.5 DISCOVERING HIDDEN PASSIONS AND INTERESTS

Imagine a canvas stretched out before you, blank yet brimming with potential. Retirement offers a similar landscape, inviting you to explore hidden passions and interests that may have been overshadowed by the demands of daily life. Many women find themselves at this crossroads, eager yet uncertain about where to begin. The first step is to ignite a sense of curiosity about what genuinely excites you. This process starts with brainstorming sessions, where you jot down activities that have always intrigued you— whether it's painting, gardening, or learning the violin. Let your mind wander freely, without judgment or hesitation. This exercise aims to shake off the dust from interests that may have been shelved for decades, waiting patiently for their moment to shine.

Participation in introductory classes can serve as a gentle entry point into these newfound or rediscovered pursuits. Community centers, local colleges, and online platforms offer beginner courses designed to spark interest and nurture skills. These classes provide a structured environment where you can learn at your own pace, surrounded by others who share your excitement. They also serve as a fantastic opportunity to meet like-minded individuals, creating a sense of camaraderie and support. For instance, a pottery class might reveal a natural talent for sculpting, while a photography workshop could reignite a forgotten passion for capturing life's moments. By stepping into these spaces, you open yourself to a world of possibilities, each offering its own unique set of rewards.

Experimentation is key, and this requires courage and a willingness to step outside your comfort zone. The idea is to sample a variety of activities, much like sampling dishes at a buffet, to discover what truly resonates with you. Local workshops and community events often provide hands-on experiences without the commitment of long-term enrollment. These settings allow you to dabble in different hobbies, from salsa dancing to woodworking, without the pressure of mastering them immediately. This process uncovers hidden talents and fosters personal growth. Engaging in these activities can lead to unexpected transformations, as many individuals find a renewed sense of purpose and confidence through hobby exploration. Whether it turns into a lifelong passion or a brief flirtation, each new endeavor adds to the rich mixture of your personal development.

Consider the joy of rediscovering past interests that may have been set aside during your career. Perhaps you once loved to write poetry or play the piano but haven't touched a pen or a key in years. Retirement provides the perfect opportunity to revisit these activities with fresh eyes and renewed enthusiasm. Reconnecting with childhood pastimes can be particularly rewarding, as they often carry a sense of nostalgia and comfort. They remind us of simpler times when creativity flowed freely, unencumbered by the responsibilities of adulthood. By revisiting these interests, you honor your past and enrich your present. They offer a delightful way to fill your days with activities that bring joy and satisfaction.

As you navigate this exploration, keep in mind that discovering hidden passions is not about achieving perfection or even proficiency. It's about finding joy in the process, embracing curiosity, and allowing yourself the freedom to explore without judgment. This stage of life offers the rare gift of time—time to experiment, to play, and to indulge in activities that nurture your soul. Whether you find yourself drawn to painting landscapes, writing memoirs, or simply taking nature walks, let these pursuits guide you toward a fulfilling and engaged lifestyle. The possibilities are endless, each offering its own path to personal enrichment.

1.6 PERSONALITY ASSESSMENTS: TOOLS FOR SELFDISCOVERY

Imagine having a detailed map that helps you navigate the intricate landscape of your personality, allowing you to uncover layers of yourself you might not have fully understood. Personality assessments offer just that—a tool to delve into the nuances of your character, preferences, and potential. These assessments, like the Myers-Briggs Type Indicator (MBTI) and the Enneagram, provide insights into your personality traits, helping you appreciate your innate strengths and areas for growth. The MBTI categorizes personalities into 16 distinct types based on factors like introversion versus extroversion, while the Enneagram identifies nine interconnected personality types. Understanding these can illuminate why you gravitate toward certain activities or how you approach decision-making. This newfound clarity can be a catalyst for self-acceptance and personal development.

Once you've completed an assessment, the next step is interpreting the results in a meaningful and actionable way. It's not just about reading a report; it's about understanding how the results translate into real-world applications. Consider using worksheets that map your personality traits to potential interests and activities. For example, exploring artistic pursuits or problem-solving workshops might be fulfilling if your assessment reveals a strong preference for creativity and innovation. Community-building activities or group classes could be a perfect fit if you thrive on social interaction. These tools encourage a deeper engagement with your results, transforming abstract concepts into concrete actions that align with your personality.

Understanding your personality can serve as a guidepost when choosing new pursuits, ensuring that your post-retirement activities are both rewarding and aligned with who you are. Take, for instance, someone who discovers through the Enneagram that they are a Type 2, known for their nurturing nature and desire to help others. This insight could lead them to volunteer work in caregiving or mentorship, where they can thrive by supporting and nurturing those around them. By aligning activities with your personality traits, you create a harmonious balance between your inherent tendencies and the new roles you embrace. This alignment often leads to greater satisfaction and a sense of authenticity in your daily life.

Integrating these personality insights into your daily routine is where the real transformation occurs. Knowing your personality type can inform how you structure your day, interact with others, and approach challenges. For instance, an introverted personality might find solace in quiet mornings filled with reflective activities, while an extroverted personality might thrive by scheduling social interactions throughout the day. Tailoring your routines to suit your personality enhances your well-being and optimizes your energy levels and productivity. This personalized approach allows you to engage with the world in a natural and fulfilling way, reducing stress and increasing joy.

Consider famous examples of individuals who have leveraged their personality insights to achieve remarkable things. Think of an artist who, understanding her need for solitude, structured her day around quiet mornings of painting, leading to some of her most profound work. Or a community leader whose extroverted nature drove him to organize successful local events, bringing people together in meaningful ways. These stories remind us that when we honor our personality traits, we unlock potential and possibilities that might otherwise remain dormant.

As you explore the depths of your personality, remember that these assessments are just one part of a larger picture. They provide a foundation for building a life that resonates with your true self. Embrace their insights and allow them to guide you toward activities and roles that fulfill and inspire you.

1.7 CRAFTING YOUR UNIQUE RETIREMENT NARRATIVE

Imagine your life as a book, with each chapter detailing the experiences, lessons, and triumphs that have shaped your journey. Retirement is not the end of this story but the beginning of a new chapter—a blank page ready for your unique narrative. The power of storytelling lies in its ability to clarify and amplify our experiences, offering insight into our past and guiding our future. Writing your retirement story can be a transformative exercise, allowing you to reflect on your life's journey and envision what lies ahead. Start by considering the key moments that have defined your path thus far. What lessons have you learned? What dreams remain unfulfilled? Use these reflections as the foundation for your narrative, crafting a story that captures your hopes, aspirations, and the essence of who you are.

Narrative writing exercises can help you articulate your personal retirement story. Begin by writing a letter to your future self, detailing your vision for this next phase of life. What do you hope to achieve? How do you envision spending your days? This exercise encourages you to think deeply about your goals and aspirations, providing a roadmap for the future. Another approach is to write a short story featuring yourself as the main character. Picture a day in your ideal retirement filled with activities that bring joy and fulfillment. Describe the scenes, characters, and emotions in vivid detail, painting a picture of the life you wish to create. These exercises help you clarify your vision and inspire you to take action toward realizing it.

The power of storytelling extends beyond personal growth; it also fosters connection and inspiration when shared with others. Sharing your narrative opens the door to meaningful conversations, allowing others to learn from your experiences and insights. Consider joining platforms or groups where you can share your story, such as writing clubs, online forums, or community storytelling events. These spaces provide a supportive environment to express your journey, offering encouragement and feedback from like-minded individuals. Sharing your story can also be a source of inspiration for others, demonstrating that retirement is a time of opportunity and growth.

Documenting your journey through journaling or blogging can be a valuable tool for reflection and growth. Keeping a record of your experiences allows you to track your progress, celebrate achievements, and learn from challenges. Writing provides a private space to express thoughts and emotions, offering clarity and perspective. Regular entries can help you stay connected to your goals, fostering a sense of accountability. For those who enjoy a more public platform, blogging offers the chance to share your journey with a broader audience. Blogs can serve as a personal diary and a resource for others seeking guidance and inspiration. Whether you choose to journal privately or blog publicly, documenting your experiences ensures that your narrative continues to evolve and inspire.

1.8 STORYTELLING FRAMEWORK: CRAFTING YOUR PERSONAL NARRATIVE

Consider using a storytelling framework to structure your retirement narrative. Start by identifying the theme or message you wish to convey. Next, outline the key events or experiences that have shaped your journey. Finally, describe your vision for the future, highlighting the goals and aspirations that drive you. Use this framework as a guide to craft a narrative that captures the essence of your retirement story.

In crafting your unique retirement narrative, you create a powerful tool for personal growth and connection. Your story is a reflection of your journey, capturing the challenges you've overcome and the dreams you hold dear. As you embrace this new chapter, allow your narrative to guide and inspire you, reminding you of the endless possibilities that lie ahead. Retirement is not just a phase of life; it's an opportunity to write the next chapter of your story, filled with purpose, joy, and fulfillment.

2

FINANCIAL PEACE OF MIND WITHOUT HIGH WEALTH

Picture this: Joan, a vibrant 62-year-old, sits at her kitchen table, surrounded by a pile of bills and receipts. She looks at her retirement savings account with a mix of hope and trepidation. Like many women in her age group, Joan is navigating the complex waters of retirement finances, keen to maintain her lifestyle without the cushion of a lavish pension. This chapter is dedicated to women like Joan, who seek financial peace of mind without relying on substantial wealth. It's about creating a roadmap that leads to comfort and security, allowing you to enjoy the fruits of your labor without unnecessary stress.

2.1 BUDGETING FOR A COMFORTABLE LIFESTYLE

Effective budgeting is at the heart of financial peace—a skill that can transform how you manage money during retirement. Envision your budget as a well-crafted recipe, where each ingredient is carefully measured to create a satisfying dish. Begin by understanding the foundational elements of a sustainable retirement budget, which includes distinguishing between fixed and variable expenses. Fixed expenses are your essentials, such as housing, utilities, and healthcare, which remain relatively stable each month. Variable expenses, on the other hand, cover discretionary spending like dining out, travel, and hobbies, which can fluctuate based on your choices.

Tracking these expenses is crucial; thankfully, technology offers several tools to simplify this task. Consider using budgeting apps like YNAB (You Need A Budget) or EveryDollar, which help you monitor spending and make informed financial decisions. These apps provide a user-friendly platform to categorize expenses and visualize your financial landscape. For those who prefer a more traditional approach, spreadsheets can be equally effective, allowing you to customize and adjust as needed. The key is consistency—regularly updating your budget ensures you stay on track and avoid surprises.

Prioritizing needs over wants is essential in crafting a budget that supports a comfortable lifestyle. This involves distinguishing between what's necessary and what's merely desirable. Practical exercises, such as categorizing expenses into "needs" and "wants," can clarify where your money goes and where adjustments can be made. Start by listing all monthly expenses, then assess each item's importance. This exercise not only highlights potential savings but also encourages mindful spending, ensuring your resources align with your values and goals.

Regular budget reviews and adjustments are vital to maintaining financial stability. Life is dynamic, and so should your budget be. Schedule regular strategy sessions—perhaps quarterly or semiannually—to review your financial situation and make necessary adjustments. This practice allows you to adapt to life changes, such as unexpected medical expenses or shifts in income. During these reviews, assess if your spending aligns with your priorities and if there are areas where you can cut back. Flexibility is your ally, enabling you to respond to financial challenges with confidence and ease.

Living comfortably within your means doesn't mean sacrificing joy or fulfillment. It's about making thoughtful choices that support your desired lifestyle. Consider cost-saving tips like bulk purchasing or energy-saving practices, which can reduce expenses without diminishing your quality of life. For instance, buying nonperishable items in bulk can lead to significant savings over time. Similarly, simple measures like unplugging electronics when not in use or switching to LED lighting can lower utility bills. These strategies demonstrate how minor adjustments can impact your overall budget, allowing you to enjoy retirement with peace of mind.

Practical Exercise: Crafting Your Budget

Take a moment to draft a preliminary budget. List your expenses, such as mortgage or rent, utilities, and insurance. Next, add your variable expenses, like groceries, entertainment, and travel. Use a budgeting app or spreadsheet to categorize and track these expenses over the next month. At the end of the month, review your spending. Identify areas where you can reduce costs and adjust your budget accordingly. This exercise enhances financial awareness and empowers you to make informed decisions, fostering a sense of control and confidence in your financial future.

2.2 SMART SAVING STRATEGIES: MAXIMIZING YOUR INCOME

Imagine a rainy day. The sky darkens, and the gentle patter of raindrops turns into a steady downpour. In financial terms, these unexpected storms are the unforeseen expenses that can unsettle even the most carefully laid plans. Building an emergency fund is like an umbrella for such days—it's your safety net, protecting you from life's unpredictable turns. To establish this fund, calculate three to six months' worth of living expenses. Consider all necessary costs like housing, food, and healthcare. Once you've determined the amount, gradually set aside money until you reach your target. Begin with small, consistent contributions. For example, directly allocate a fixed percentage of any extra income, like tax refunds or bonuses, into your emergency fund. This method ensures you are prepared to face financial challenges with resilience and confidence.

The concept of automatic savings is another invaluable strategy to secure your financial future. Think of it as setting your financial autopilot. By setting up automatic transfers to your savings account, you remove the temptation to spend money on nonessential items. This approach ensures that savings become a priority rather than an afterthought. To implement this, coordinate with your bank to transfer a predetermined amount from your checking account to your savings account each month. Even small amounts add up over time, contributing to a sense of financial stability and peace of mind. This practice simplifies the saving process and cultivates a habit of consistent saving, reinforcing your commitment to financial health.

Though seemingly negligible, daily expenses can accumulate into significant costs over time. By adopting smart strategies, you can reduce these expenses without compromising your quality of life.

Start by embracing couponing and discount shopping. Many retailers offer loyalty programs and coupons, which can lead to substantial savings on everyday purchases. Additionally, consider shopping during sales or exploring generic brands, which often provide similar quality at a lower price. Another effective way to trim costs is through conservation. Turning off lights when leaving a room or using energy-efficient appliances can significantly reduce utility bills. These small changes can lead to noticeable savings, allowing you to allocate funds toward more meaningful endeavors.

Managing and reducing debt is a critical component of maximizing your income. Debt can often feel like a heavy weight, restricting your financial freedom. To address this, create a debt repayment plan. Start by listing all your debts, including interest rates and minimum payments. Prioritize paying off high-interest debts first, as they accumulate the most cost over time. Consider using the snowball method, where you focus on paying off the smallest debt first, then roll the amount into the next smallest debt, creating a momentum that motivates continued progress. Alternatively, the avalanche method targets high-interest debts first for quicker financial relief. Whichever method you choose, the goal is to chip away at your debt consistently, freeing up more income for savings and investments. By actively managing your debt, you can reduce financial stress and create a more straightforward path toward achieving your retirement dreams.

Incorporating these smart saving strategies into your financial routine ensures that you make the most of your resources, regardless of the size of your retirement fund. Whether it's setting up automatic savings, reducing daily expenses, or tackling debt, each step contributes to a more secure and fulfilling retirement. As you implement these practices, you'll find that financial peace is not just about having a significant income but about making wise and deliberate choices with your resources.

2.3 AFFORDABLE INVESTMENT OPTIONS FOR BEGINNERS

Stepping into the world of investing can feel like entering a bustling market with endless stalls, each offering promises of prosperity. For many women approaching or already in retirement, the idea of investing may seem daunting, especially with limited resources. Yet, the landscape of investing has evolved, offering numerous options that are both accessible and affordable. Picture investing as planting a garden: it requires patience, care, and a bit of knowledge about where to place your seeds. One of the most beginner-friendly investment options is low-cost index funds or Exchange-Traded Funds (ETFs). These funds pool money from many investors to purchase a diversified portfolio of stocks or bonds, mirroring a specific index like the S&P 500. By investing in these funds, you're buying into a broad market, which reduces the risk associated with individual stocks. With low expense ratios, these funds are an efficient way to grow your money over time without the need for constant management.

Diversification, a cornerstone of investing, is a safety net for your portfolio. Pretend you are walking a tightrope with a balancing pole; diversification helps you maintain equilibrium by spreading investments across various assets. This strategy mitigates risk because one asset's performance doesn't dictate your entire portfolio's success. A well-diversified portfolio might include a mix of stocks, bonds, and real estate, each contributing differently to your investment goals. Consider the example of a retiree who allocates her savings into a blend of domestic stocks, international bonds, and real estate investment trusts (REITs). This mixture provides stability and opens avenues for growth and income. By diversifying, you shield your investments from market volatility while positioning yourself for long-term success.

In the digital age, investment platforms have become more accessible than ever, opening doors for beginners eager to dip their toes into investing. Online brokerages, such as Robinhood or Charles Schwab, offer user-friendly interfaces with low fees, making it easier for newcomers to navigate the investment waters without feeling overwhelmed. These platforms often provide educational resources, guiding you through the basics of trading and offering insights into market trends. They also allow you to start small, with minimal initial investments, making them ideal for those new to investing. By choosing a platform that suits your comfort level and financial goals, you can begin to build a portfolio that aligns with your vision for retirement.

Starting small and growing your investments is a prudent approach, especially for those new to the investment arena. Think of it as dipping your toes in the water before diving in. This strategy, known as dollar-cost averaging, involves investing a fixed amount of money at regular intervals, regardless of market conditions. By doing so, you buy more shares when prices are low and fewer when prices are high, which can lower the average cost of your investments over time. This method builds discipline and reduces the emotional impact of market fluctuations. Additionally, reinvesting dividends—profits paid out by companies to shareholders—can significantly boost your portfolio's growth. By choosing to reinvest these earnings, you purchase more shares, compounding your investment's growth over time. This approach ensures that your money continues to work for you, even when you're not actively managing it.

As you explore these affordable investment options, remember that investing is a journey of learning and adaptation. It's about finding what works for you and aligning your investments with your financial goals. Start with the basics, embrace the learning process, and gradually expand your investment knowledge. With time, patience, and a bit of curiosity, you'll find that investing can be a rewarding venture that supports a fulfilling and secure retirement.

2.4 NAVIGATING SOCIAL SECURITY AND BENEFITS

Social Security, a foundation of retirement planning, often feels like a complex maze. Yet, understanding its fundamentals can provide a sense of security. Social Security is a government program designed to replace a portion of your income when you retire. Your benefits are calculated based on your 35 highest earning years. If you worked fewer than 35 years, zeros are factored into the calculation, which can lower your average earnings and, subsequently, your benefits. To qualify, you generally need 40 credits, which you earn through paying Social Security taxes on your earnings. Most people accumulate these credits by working for at least ten years. Once you've reached the eligible age of 62, you can start claiming benefits. However, claiming early results in reduced monthly payouts. Full retirement age varies between 66 and 67, depending on your birth year. Waiting until 70 maximizes your monthly benefits, though not everyone can afford to wait that long.

The application process for claiming Social Security benefits is more straightforward than you might think. The Social Security Administration (SSA) offers an online application that guides you through each step. You'll need personal information, such as your Social Security number, birth certificate, and the names of your spouse and children. It's also wise to gather financial documents, including tax returns, to streamline the process. Once your application is submitted, the SSA will review your information and notify you of your benefit status. Many find the online process convenient, as it allows for tracking progress and receiving updates electronically. If you prefer in-person assistance, visiting a local Social

Security office is also an option. However, making an appointment is advisable to avoid long wait times.

Timing is everything when it comes to maximizing your Social Security benefits. One key strategy is delaying your claim. Each year you wait beyond your full retirement age, your benefits increase by a certain percentage until you reach 70. This delay can significantly enhance your monthly income if you have other resources to rely on in the interim. Another approach involves considering spousal benefits. If you're married, divorced, or widowed, you may be eligible for benefits based on your spouse's work record, potentially boosting your overall income. Consulting with a financial advisor can help determine the best strategy for your specific circumstances, ensuring you optimize your benefits based on your unique life situation.

Beyond Social Security, several other programs can support retirees, enhancing financial stability. Medicare, a federal health insurance program, becomes available at age 65, providing coverage for hospital stays, doctor visits, and prescription medications. Understanding the different parts of Medicare—Part A, B, C, and D—can help you choose a plan that suits your healthcare needs. Another government program, Medicaid, assists low income individuals with medical expenses, supplementing Medicare for those who qualify. Numerous low-income assistance programs also offer support for necessities like food, housing, and energy. These programs can make a substantial difference in your financial well-being, providing relief and peace of mind.

To navigate these benefits effectively, staying informed and proactive is essential. Regularly reviewing your Social Security statement, available online, can help you understand your estimated benefits and plan accordingly. This statement provides a snapshot of your earnings history and the credits you've accumulated, allowing you to verify the accuracy of your records. Additionally, attending workshops or seminars on retirement planning can offer valuable insights into managing your benefits and maximizing your income. These resources empower you to make informed decisions, ensuring that you leverage every available opportunity to secure a comfortable retirement.

2.5 FINANCIAL PLANNING FOR DIVERSE SITUATIONS

Retirement brings a diverse set of financial circumstances for everyone, shaped significantly by personal and family dynamics. Whether you're navigating this phase as a single woman, part of a couple, or within a family structure that includes dependents, your financial planning must reflect these nuances. For singles, the focus often leans towards self-reliance and ensuring that savings and investments cater to individual needs. This might involve a heavier emphasis on building a robust emergency fund and providing comprehensive healthcare coverage. In contrast, couples must navigate joint finances, balancing shared expenses while also accounting for each partner's individual financial goals. This requires open communication and joint decision-making, particularly when planning for large expenditures or long-term care. Families with dependents, such as children or elderly parents, face the added complexity of supporting multiple generations. This can include budgeting for education costs or healthcare needs, requiring careful prioritization and potentially more significant savings goals to accommodate these additional responsibilities.

The unpredictable nature of life means that even the best-laid plans can face disruption. A contingency plan is paramount, whether it is a sudden health issue or an unexpected family event. Start by identifying potential risks and considering how they might impact your financial situation. This could be anything from medical emergencies to natural disasters. Once you've pinpointed these risks, consider the resources you would need to mitigate them. For instance, maintaining a dedicated emergency fund that can cover several months of expenses is a practical step. Additionally, consider your insurance policies—do they adequately cover the potential scenarios you've identified? Ensure your policies are up-to-date and you understand your coverage's specifics. Regularly revisiting these plans ensures they remain relevant as your life circumstances evolve.

Customizing your financial plan to fit your unique situation is crucial. A one-size-fits-all approach rarely works because everyone's financial landscape is different. Use financial worksheets or outlines to map out your specific needs and objectives. These tools help you visualize your financial picture, allowing you to identify areas where adjustments are necessary. For example, if you're experiencing a lifestyle change, such as downsizing your home, your financial plan should reflect this shift. Tailored strategies include reallocating funds to better serve your new goals, whether increasing your savings rate or investing in a new opportunity. The key is regularly reviewing and updating your plan to align with your current and future aspirations.

Seeking professional financial advice can also be wise, especially when navigating complex situations or significant life changes occur. Financial advisors bring expertise that can help you optimize your strategy and ensure you're making informed decisions. When choosing an advisor, look for someone with a solid reputation and relevant experience, ideally someone who understands your specific needs and goals. It's important to ask questions about their approach and ensure you feel comfortable with their advice. Many advisors offer a free initial consultation, which can be a good opportunity to assess whether their services align with your expectations. Remember, the goal is to find a partner in your financial planning who can provide clarity and confidence in your retirement strategy.

2.6 CREATIVE WAYS TO SUPPLEMENT YOUR INCOME

As retirement unfolds, the rhythm of daily life changes and opportunities arise to explore new avenues for financial growth. Parttime work and flexible job opportunities are increasingly tailored to fit a retiree's lifestyle, offering the chance to engage with the world while supplementing income. Consider roles in freelancing or consultancy, where your accumulated expertise can be leveraged without the constraints of a full-time role. These positions allow you to work on projects that excite you from the comfort of your home or in settings that suit you. Alternatively, seasonal or part-time employment can provide a steady yet flexible income stream. For instance, working as a seasonal tour guide or a parttime retail assistant during busy periods can add variety to your routine while enhancing your financial stability. These roles provide financial benefits and enhance social interaction, allowing you to remain active and engaged in community life.

Your skills and hobbies, honed over a lifetime, can also become a source of income. Teaching or tutoring in a specialized field allows you to share your knowledge and passion with others. Whether it's offering piano lessons to children or guiding adults through the intricacies of a new language, teaching can be as rewarding financially as it is personally fulfilling. Moreover, the digital age offers platforms that make it easy to reach students worldwide, broadening your impact and income potential. For those with a knack for creativity, selling crafts or homemade goods online presents a lucrative opportunity. Websites like Etsy provide a marketplace for handmade items, enabling you to turn crafting hobbies into a thriving business. Whether you create jewelry, knitwear or home decor, there's a growing market eager to embrace unique, handcrafted items. This venture supplements income and allows you to express creativity and connect with a community of like-minded artisans.

Passive income opportunities offer another path, one that requires minimal ongoing effort but can yield considerable benefits. Renting out property or space, for instance, can be an excellent way to generate extra income. If you have a spare room, consider listing it on short-term rental sites like Airbnb. Renting out unused storage space or parking areas can also provide a steady income stream for those with unused storage space. Once set up, these arrangements typically require minimal effort, allowing you to enjoy financial returns with low day-to-day involvement. The key to successful passive income is initial planning and setup, after which your assets continue to work for you.

The digital landscape also opens doors to community and online resources that support income generation. Platforms like Fiverr offer a space to promote your freelance services, whether it's graphic design, writing, or digital marketing. These platforms connect you with clients seeking your particular skill set, providing a flexible approach to work that fits your schedule and interests. Joining online marketplaces is another way to reach a wider audience and diversify income opportunities. Notably, these platforms often come with built-in tools for marketing and sales, reducing the need for extensive technical knowledge. This accessibility means you can focus on your strengths and passions, allowing your talents to shine in a global marketplace.

Incorporating these creative income strategies into your retirement plan provides not only financial rewards but also personal satisfaction. By exploring part-time work, leveraging your skills, and tapping into passive income opportunities, you create a diverse financial portfolio that supports a vibrant lifestyle. As we transition to the next chapter, we'll continue to build on these foundations, exploring how to maintain a fulfilling and active retirement that aligns with your goals and aspirations.

3

BUILDING AND MAINTAINING SOCIAL CONNECTIONS

Gazing out your window, you might observe the lively flow of life and wonder how to reconnect with its vibrant social threads. Retirement brings the luxury of time, yet it can also introduce a feeling of isolation, a stark shift from the familiar, interaction-rich environment of work to a quieter, more individual lifestyle. This chapter guides you towards rediscovering your sense of community—finding a group that resonates with your interests and lays the groundwork for enduring supportive relationships. It encourages you to venture beyond your usual boundaries, to engage with clubs or groups that bring you joy, and to relish the collective experiences that come from such engagement. On this path of reconnection, you will find the unmatched joy of being part of a community that shares your interests and celebrates life's achievements together.

Joining clubs and groups is like opening the door to a world of camaraderie and support. When you become part of a community, you gain more than just companionship; you find a place to share stories, laughter, and common interests. This sense of belonging can profoundly enhance your social life, providing a network of friends who understand your joys and challenges. Whether it's a book club that meets over coffee or a gardening group that exchanges tips and stories, these gatherings foster connections and kindle friendships that enrich your retirement years. Sharing experiences with others who share your passions can transform ordinary days into extraordinary ones filled with warmth and understanding.

Finding the right club or group starts with identifying what ignites your passion. Contemplate exploring local community centers or libraries, which often host a variety of clubs catering to diverse interests. From knitting or quilting circles to photography classes, these venues offer a treasure trove of activities that can spark joy and engagement. Libraries frequently serve as hubs for educational and social events, providing a welcoming space to meet new people and learn new things. For those who prefer a more tailored approach, online platforms like Meetup offer a gateway to niche groups that align with your personal values and interests. Whether you're drawn to hiking, art, or culinary delights, these platforms connect you with like-minded individuals eager to share their enthusiasm.

The variety of clubs and groups available is as diverse as your interests. Book clubs offer a chance to delve into new worlds through literature, while gardening groups provide the satisfaction of nurturing life and sharing the fruits of your labor. Art classes let you explore creativity and self-expression, offering a supportive environment to try new techniques and hone your skills. Each group provides a unique opportunity to expand your horizons and form connections based on shared passions. Joining these clubs fills your calendar with engaging activities and introduces you to a community of individuals who enrich your experience with diverse perspectives and stories.

Active participation in these groups is key to fostering deeper connections. Attending meetings is a start, but taking an active role can transform your experience. Volunteering for leadership roles or organizing group activities allows you to shape the group's direction and create memorable events. By stepping into these roles, you contribute to the group's success and strengthen your ties with fellow members. Organizing a book club meeting or planning a garden tour encourages collaboration and creativity, strengthening bonds and a sense of accomplishment. Active involvement ensures you are not just a spectator but an integral part of your community, where your contributions are valued and friendships flourish.

Reflection Exercise: Mapping Your Social Interests

Think about taking a moment to reflect on your interests. Grab a pen and paper and list activities you've always wanted to try or deepen your involvement. Think about the skills you have and how they might contribute to a club or group. Reflect on what you hope to gain from these interactions—whether it's learning something new, meeting new people, or simply enjoying a hobby. This exercise helps you identify potential paths and set intentions for building meaningful social connections.

Finding your tribe adds a vibrant layer to your retirement, offering companionship and a sense of purpose. As you explore these connections, you'll discover that being part of a community brings a wealth of experiences, friendships, and opportunities for growth. Welcome the chance to join clubs and groups and watch as your social circle expands, enveloping you in a warm embrace of shared interests and joyful interactions.

3.1 VIRTUAL COMMUNITIES: CONNECTING IN THE DIGITAL AGE

Regard the digital landscape, a vibrant realm where friendships blossom and communities thrive, all from the comfort of your home. Virtual communities have become a lifeline for many, offering a space to connect, share, and grow beyond geographical constraints. In today's world, platforms like Facebook and LinkedIn serve as gateways to these digital circles, providing a space where you can engage with others who share your interests and passions. Whether it's a Facebook group dedicated to gardening or a LinkedIn community for lifelong learners, these platforms foster a sense of belonging and connection that transcends physical boundaries. Through digital interaction, you can participate in conversations, share experiences, and build relationships with people from all corners of the globe, enriching your social life in ways you might not have considered.

Selecting the right online platform is crucial to maximizing the benefits of virtual communities. Start by giving thought to your interests and the type of interaction you seek. Are you looking for professional networking, casual socializing, or a mix of both? Platforms with user-friendly interfaces can make your online experience more enjoyable and less daunting. For instance, Facebook's intuitive design allows you to easily navigate through groups, while LinkedIn offers a more structured environment for professional engagement. Interest-based communities provide tailored spaces where you can delve into specific topics, whether it's a niche hobby or a broader subject like wellness. Evaluating these features will help you find a platform that aligns with your preferences, ensuring a fulfilling and engaging experience.

Digital connections offer unparalleled flexibility and accessibility, enabling you to maintain friendships and participate in activities regardless of your location. You can join global interest groups that connect you with people who share your passions, learn from diverse perspectives, and stay updated on the latest trends. Virtual meetups and webinars allow you to attend events and workshops from your living room, offering opportunities for learning and interaction without the need for travel. This convenience means that you can engage with your community on your terms, fitting social activities around your schedule and commitments. Whether participating in a virtual book club or attending a live cooking class, the digital world opens doors to experiences that keep your social life dynamic and enriching.

As you navigate these digital spaces, it's essential to prioritize your privacy and security. Social media platforms offer various privacy controls that help protect your personal information. Take the time to familiarize yourself with these settings, adjusting them to suit your comfort level. Ensure your profile is visible only to those you trust and be cautious about sharing sensitive information. Engaging with content thoughtfully and staying informed about platform features can also enhance your online experience. Regularly reviewing your privacy settings and understanding how to report inappropriate content are proactive steps that empower you to stay safe online. By maintaining these safeguards, you can enjoy the benefits of virtual communities while protecting your digital footprint.

3.2 MAINTAINING LONG-DISTANCE FRIENDSHIPS

Imagine the joy of hearing the voice of an old friend, the laughter bridging the miles between you. In retirement, nurturing longdistance friendships becomes even more vital. These connections offer a sense of continuity and comfort, reminding you of shared memories and experiences. Regular phone calls or video chats can rekindle the warmth of those relationships, allowing you to share stories, offer support, and celebrate milestones together. A simple call can turn an ordinary day into a special one, bringing familiar voices and cherished moments into your home. Establishing a routine for these calls—perhaps a weekly or bi-weekly chat— creates anticipation and maintains the bond that distance might otherwise strain.

Overcoming the barriers of distance requires creativity and intention. While technology offers many solutions, receiving a handwritten letter or a thoughtfully curated care package is profoundly personal. These tangible tokens of friendship carry a piece of your presence, a reminder of the connection that transcends miles. Visualize the delight of opening a package filled with favorite teas, a book you both discussed, or a small craft you made. Such gestures speak volumes, reinforcing that your friend holds a special place in your heart despite the distance. Additionally, coordinating virtual activities like movie nights or book discussions can bridge the gap, creating shared experiences that mimic those enjoyed in person. Selecting a film to watch simultaneously or reading the same novel opens avenues for conversation and shared reflection.

In today's digital age, technology serves as both a bridge and a lifeline for maintaining friendships separated by geography. Apps like WhatsApp or Skype make it easy to stay in touch through text, voice, and video calls. These tools allow you to see each other's expressions, hear the nuances in your voices, and engage in real time dialogue. They foster an immediacy and intimacy that letter writing alone cannot capture. Whether it's a spontaneous video call to share a recent happening or a planned conversation to catch up on each other's lives, these platforms keep the lines of communication open and dynamic. They enable you to celebrate birthdays, holidays, and even daily victories together, nurturing the friendship with regular interaction.

Shared experiences create lasting memories and deepen connections, even when friends are miles apart. Planning joint vacations or meetups can turn anticipation into reality, providing opportunities to explore new places and enjoy each other's company. Picture a weekend getaway to a charming town you've always wanted to visit or a reunion at a favorite vacation spot. These trips become more than just a chance to see each other; they are adventures that build new memories, enhancing the fabric of your friendship. Even if such visits are infrequent, the planning and anticipation can keep the friendship vibrant and engaging, offering a goal to look forward to and a reward for the patience and effort invested in maintaining the relationship. By blending technology with personal gestures and shared experiences, your long-distance friendships can flourish, providing joy, support, and continuity throughout your retirement years.

3.3 HOSTING GATHERINGS: BRINGING PEOPLE TOGETHER

Imagine the warmth of a room filled with laughter, the clinking of glasses, and the soft hum of conversation. Hosting gatherings is more than just bringing people together; it's about weaving a tapestry of relationships that can enrich your life. Opening your home to friends and neighbors creates a hub of connection and camaraderie. These gatherings build a network of local friends, offering a sense of community that many retirees seek. Hosting allows you to rekindle old friendships while forging new ones, transforming acquaintances into lifelong companions. It's not just about the event itself but the lasting bonds formed that continue to grow and flourish over time.

Planning a successful gathering requires creativity and organization, ensuring everyone feels welcome and included. Consider hosting theme-based parties, which can add an element of excitement and cohesiveness to your gathering. Whether it's a 70s disco night or a tropical luau, themes encourage guests to engage and participate actively. Potlucks are another great option, allowing everyone to contribute a dish and share in the communal experience. This eases the burden of preparation and introduces a delightful variety of flavors and dishes. Setting a comfortable and welcoming atmosphere is key; think ambient lighting, cozy seating arrangements, and background music that encourages conversation. Small touches like these create an inviting environment where guests feel at ease.

Let your creativity shine when planning events that are memorable and unique. An outdoor picnic on a sunny afternoon can offer a refreshing change from indoor gatherings, allowing guests to enjoy nature while socializing. Reflect on organizing a game night where friendly competition and laughter can break the ice and strengthen bonds. These unique gatherings entertain and provide an opportunity for guests to interact in different settings, fostering more profound connections. Encourage guests to bring along games or activities they enjoy, creating a collaborative atmosphere that enhances the experience. The key is to encourage creative thinking and tailor events to the interests and preferences of your friends, ensuring a personalized and memorable gathering.

Regularly hosting events can sustain and nurture relationships, keeping friendships vibrant and active. Establishing a routine, such as monthly or quarterly gatherings, creates a rhythm that friends can look forward to, providing continuity and anticipation. These regular meet-ups serve as touchpoints, allowing friends to catch up, share updates, and strengthen bonds. Over time, these gatherings become cherished traditions, etched into the social calendar. They offer a sense of stability and belonging, where everyone knows they have a place to connect and unwind. By committing to regular hosting, you cultivate a supportive network that enriches your retirement and ensures your social circle remains lively and engaged.

The process of hosting and planning these gatherings is as rewarding as the events themselves. It provides an opportunity to express your personality and creativity, whether through the choice of theme, menu, or decorations. Moreover, it allows you to practice and refine organizational, communication, and hospitality skills. As you plan each event, you'll become more adept at anticipating the needs and preferences of your guests, ensuring that each gathering is a success. This sense of accomplishment is deeply satisfying, reinforcing the value and importance of maintaining social connections.

3.4 EMBRACING VOLUNTEERISM: GIVING BACK AND MAKING FRIENDS

Envision standing shoulder to shoulder with a group of enthusiastic individuals, all united by a common goal to make a difference. Volunteering provides a unique opportunity to give back to your community and forge meaningful connections. Engaging in community service projects immerses you in environments where camaraderie and collaboration thrive. These settings offer fertile ground for developing friendships based on shared values and experiences. Whether painting a community center, organizing a charity event, or mentoring young students, each act of service brings you closer to others equally passionate about creating positive change.

For retirees, the benefits of volunteering extend far beyond the immediate impact on society. It's a powerful way to rediscover a sense of purpose and belonging, which can sometimes wane after leaving the workforce. Volunteering fills your days with meaningful activities that engage you mentally and physically. The satisfaction derived from contributing to the well-being of others fosters a profound sense of fulfillment. This active participation in community life can significantly enhance your emotional wellbeing as you witness firsthand the results of your efforts and the smiles on the faces of those you help. Moreover, volunteering often introduces you to diverse groups of people, enriching your social circle with new friendships and perspectives.

Finding the right volunteer opportunity involves aligning your skills and interests with the needs of the community. Weigh starting with local charities, hospitals, or schools, as these organizations often seek volunteers for a variety of roles. Think about what you enjoy and where your strengths lie. Are you passionate about education? Mentoring students or assisting in a literacy program would be rewarding. If you have a knack for organization, helping with event planning or administrative tasks might suit you. By selecting roles that resonate with your interests, you will more likely find satisfaction and joy in your volunteer work. Take the time to research different organizations and visit them if possible. This allows you to get a feel for their environment and culture, ensuring a good fit for your talents and enthusiasm.

Once you're involved in a volunteer group, building connections with fellow volunteers enhances the experience. Participation in team-building activities strengthens the group dynamic and fosters trust and collaboration. These activities include workshops, training sessions, or informal gatherings where volunteers can unwind and share stories. Such interactions create a sense of community within the group, where everyone works towards a common goal. Sharing personal stories and experiences is another powerful way to bond with other volunteers. These exchanges reveal the motivations and passions that drive each person, deepening mutual understanding and respect. As you open up to others, you'll find that your volunteer group becomes more than just a team—it becomes a network of friends who support and inspire one another.

Volunteering serves as a gateway to enriching social connections and fosters personal growth. When you dedicate your time to community service, you're not just positively impacting those around you; you're also infusing your life with a sense of renewed purpose and companionship. Each volunteer opportunity you accept enriches your social life, adding vibrancy and richness to your journey through retirement. The connections you forge in these settings are rooted in mutual interests and collaborative efforts, leading to meaningful and enduring friendships. These friendships extend well beyond the confines of any single project, creating a supportive network that bolsters your social experiences and magnifies the positive impact you have within your community. Through volunteering, you engage in a reciprocal exchange—offering your skills and time while simultaneously receiving the gift of enriched social interactions and the joy of contributing to the greater good. This dynamic interplay enhances your sense of belonging and purpose, transforming volunteerism into a cornerstone of a fulfilling retirement.

3.5 INTERGENERATIONAL CONNECTIONS: LEARNING AND SHARING ACROSS AGES

Imagine sitting with your grandchildren, their eyes wide with curiosity as you share tales from your past. In return, they teach you the latest dance craze or how to navigate a new app. These moments of exchange are more than just pleasant afternoons; they are the heart of intergenerational connections. Engaging with different age groups enriches your life, offering perspectives and knowledge you might never encounter otherwise. Younger generations bring fresh ideas and insights, introducing you to technology and trends that seem daunting yet exciting. They offer a glimpse into a rapidly changing world, keeping you informed and engaged. This exchange is mutually beneficial as you pass on wisdom and life experiences, providing context and understanding that only years can bring. Sharing stories from their youth or offering career advice based on decades of experience helps them navigate their own journeys with confidence.

Creating opportunities for these intergenerational exchanges can be both simple and deeply rewarding. Give thought to joining programs or workshops designed to bridge age gaps. Many communities offer intergenerational initiatives that bring together people of different ages for mutual learning and interaction. These might include tech classes where younger participants teach seniors how to use smartphones or creative workshops where skills like knitting or painting are shared. Hosting events that welcome all age groups is another avenue. Birthday parties, holiday gatherings, or even casual family dinners can become rich environments for exchange when everyone is encouraged to interact and share. These settings foster an atmosphere where everyone feels valued and included, enhancing the bonds that unite family and community.

The benefits of intergenerational connections extend beyond the immediate joy of companionship. Younger and older individuals have much to teach each other, creating a continuous loop of learning and growth. For younger people, interacting with those who have lived through different times provides historical context and perspective. They gain insight into how past challenges were overcome, learning resilience and adaptability. Meanwhile, older adults are inspired by the energy and enthusiasm of youth, which can reignite their own passions and curiosities. This dynamic enriches your personal growth, offering new angles and insights that keep you mentally agile and emotionally fulfilled.

Mentorship programs offer a structured way to deepen these connections, fostering bonds that can last a lifetime. By providing guidance and support to younger individuals, you become a beacon of knowledge and encouragement. Whether through formal programs or informal arrangements, mentoring allows you to share your expertise, helping others navigate their paths with greater ease. It's more than imparting knowledge; it's about building relationships grounded in trust and mutual respect. These bonds enrich the lives of those you mentor and your own, providing a sense of purpose and connection that transcends generations.

Intergenerational relationships are a mainstay of a vibrant, fulfilling life, offering countless opportunities for growth and connection. As you welcome these bonds, you'll find your own life enriched with new ideas, experiences, and friendships. This chapter, focused on building and maintaining social connections, highlights the importance of diverse relationships. They form the fabric of a life well-lived, providing joy, support, and continued learning. As we move forward, mull over how these connections can be nurtured and expanded, enhancing not only your retirement but the lives of those around you.

4

CREATING A FULFILLING DAILY ROUTINE

As the early morning sun casts shades of pink and gold across the sky, a realization envelops me: retirement transcends just time passing—it's an invitation to savor and celebrate each unfolding moment. This chapter of life unfurls like a blank canvas, ripe with the promise of infusing our days with the possibilities of purpose, joy, and promise. Yet, navigating the balance between peacefulness and active engagement presents its unique set of challenges. Transitioning from the rigid schedule of a career-driven existence to the freedom of an unstructured day can stir a range of emotions, from exhilaration to apprehension, in many women. It underscores the significance of crafting a daily routine that doesn't just aim for fulfillment but becomes an essential foundation for nurturing our overall well-being and happiness.

4.1 THE ART OF BALANCING RELAXATION AND ACTIVITY

Achieving a harmonious balance between relaxation and activity is fundamental to a fulfilling life, particularly as you navigate the transition into retirement. Contemplate your daily routine, where each task and pause contributes to your inner rhythm. This balance serves to skillfully direct the flow of your day—alternating between periods of activity and rest to craft a rhythm that sustains your energy and lifts your spirits. Integrating downtime into your schedule is crucial. This downtime allows your mind and body the essential opportunity to rejuvenate. Picture yourself in a serene moment with a warm cup of tea in your hands, taking the time to pause, take a deep breath, and engage in introspective reflection. These intentional pauses are the keystones in maintaining your enthusiasm for life and keeping your energy levels high throughout your day. By consciously planning these moments of rest, you ensure that each day unfolds in a balanced and meaningful way, allowing you to seize the vibrant days of retirement life with zest and joy.

Incorporating varied activities into your routine adds a layer of interest and engagement, preventing monotony. Engaging in a mix of physical and mental activities stimulates your mind and enhances your overall well-being. Think about joining a local art class or hosting a movie or game night, where you can connect with others while exploring your interests. These activities provide an outlet for creativity and social interaction, enriching your life with new experiences and friendships. Participating in community classes or workshops keeps you active and engaged, contributing to your physical health and emotional happiness.

Relaxation, however, is not merely the absence of activity; it is a deliberate practice that rejuvenates. Meditation and quiet reflection offer sanctuary from the hustle, fostering inner peace and clarity. Try incorporating short meditation sessions into your day, allowing yourself to return to the present moment. Techniques such as deep breathing exercises can further reduce stress and promote serenity. Imagine closing your eyes, taking a deep breath, and feeling tension melt away with each exhale. These moments of stillness are invaluable, providing a foundation of serenity upon which to build your day.

Adaptability is a crucial component of a fulfilling routine, ensuring that your schedule remains flexible and responsive to your needs. Life is fluid and so should your daily activities be. Listen to your body and mind, adjusting your plans based on your energy levels and mood. There will be days when you feel invigorated and ready to tackle new challenges and others when you crave quiet and reflection. Embrace this variability, allowing yourself the grace to shift gears as needed. By honoring your natural rhythms, you craft a routine that supports your well-being and enhances your quality of life.

Interactive Exercise: Crafting Your Daily Balance

Take a moment to reflect on your current daily routine. Identify the activities that invigorate you and those that calm you. Create a simple chart listing these activities under two columns: "Energizing" and "Relaxing." Review how you might balance these elements throughout your day. Use this chart as a guide to design a routine that incorporates both serenity and pursuits, ensuring a harmonious flow. Adjust as needed, keeping in mind that flexibility is key to maintaining balance and joy.

Finding this balance between tranquility and recreation cultivates a lifestyle that nurtures every aspect of one's being. Each day becomes an opportunity to engage with the world while honoring one's needs and desires. One can unlock the potential for a joyful and fulfilling retirement as one receives this art of balance, one day at a time.

4.2 MORNING RITUALS: SETTING A POSITIVE TONE FOR THE DAY

The morning, often seen as the foundation of our day, holds the power to shape our mood and productivity. Ponder waking up not to the blare of an alarm but to the gentle glow of dawn filtering through your curtains. This peaceful start sets the stage for a day filled with intention and purpose. Establishing a soothing morning routine can transform how you approach the hours ahead. By creating a space free from rush, you allow yourself the luxury of easing into the day, your mind quiet and open to possibilities. It's about beginning with intention, where each action feels deliberate and meaningful, setting a positive tone that resonates throughout your daily activities.

Consider incorporating a few simple practices that can help set a positive tone. Gentle morning stretches or a short yoga routine can awaken your body and mind, promoting flexibility and circulation. Picture yourself on a mat, moving through poses that energize and soothe, grounding you in the present moment. Follow this with a nourishing breakfast, perhaps a plate of scrambled eggs with half an avocado brimming with nutrients. This meal fuels your body and signals the beginning of a day in which health and well-being are prioritized. When performed consistently, these rituals become anchors that ground you, providing tranquility amid the day's demands.

Personalization is key to creating a morning routine that truly resonates. Each of us has unique needs and preferences, so tailor your rituals to reflect what brings you joy and peace. For some, it might be journaling, where you jot down goals or intentions for the day. Others might find solace in a quiet corner with a cup of coffee, lost in thought, or immersed in a favorite book. The goal is to craft a routine that feels as natural as breathing and aligns with your rhythm and desires. By listening to what your heart and mind crave, you create a practice that nurtures and inspires, making mornings a time you look forward to with anticipation.

Consistency in morning habits is where the magic truly unfolds. Regularity breeds familiarity, which in turn fosters comfort and ease. Establishing a fixed wake-up time can work wonders for your internal clock, improving sleep quality and ensuring you greet each day refreshed. This consistency becomes a comforting ritual; a familiar friend greets you each morning with reassurance and steadiness. As you repeat these practices, they weave into the fabric of your daily life, bolstering your resilience and enhancing your mood. Over time, the cumulative effect of a consistent morning routine manifests in greater clarity, focus, and a sense of well-being that permeates every aspect of your life.

Reflection Exercise: Crafting Your Morning Ritual

Take a moment to reflect on what you need to start your day off right. Think about activities that invigorate and soothe you, and list them on paper. Reflect on experimenting with different elements—perhaps combining stretches with a healthy breakfast or journaling with meditation or prayer. Over the next week, try incorporating these elements into your morning.

Pay attention to how each practice makes you feel and adjust as needed. This exercise allows you to create a personalized morning routine that sets a positive tone for your day, helping you step into each morning with confidence and joy.

4.3 TIME MANAGEMENT TECHNIQUES FOR RETIREES

In retirement, time becomes a vast landscape filled with possibilities yet managing it effectively can be more challenging than expected. While exciting, this newfound freedom requires a thoughtful approach to ensure each day is productive and fulfilling. Think of time management as the compass guiding you through this landscape, helping you prioritize tasks and maximize accomplishments. By identifying what's truly important, you can direct your energy towards activities that enrich your life. Prioritizing doesn't mean filling every single minute with tasks; it means recognizing what matters most and focusing on those elements. Whether it's pursuing a passion or spending time with loved ones, knowing your priorities ensures that your days are spent in alignment with your values.

Achieving this alignment calls for strategies to organize and plan your time efficiently. Give thought to using planners or digital tools to schedule activities, providing a visual roadmap of your day. These tools help you allocate time effectively, ensuring that essential tasks are completed without encroaching on moments meant for leisure or creativity. Setting daily or weekly objectives can further enhance this process, offering clear targets to work towards. By breaking larger goals into manageable pieces, you avoid feeling overwhelmed, making it easier to maintain focus and motivation. This structured approach keeps you on track and fosters a sense of accomplishment as you check off each task, reinforcing the satisfaction of a day well spent.

Beyond structuring your time, setting boundaries is crucial in protecting your personal space and ensuring that your schedule reflects your priorities. Learning to say no to non-essential commitments can be liberating, freeing you from obligations that drain your energy. It's about recognizing that your time is valuable and choosing to spend it in ways that nourish you. This might mean declining an invitation that doesn't excite you or setting limits on volunteer work. By establishing these boundaries, you carve out time for activities that genuinely fulfill you, whether enjoying a quiet afternoon with a book or exploring a new hobby. Protecting your time in this way is an act of self-care, creating space for rest and rejuvenation.

Regularly reviewing and adjusting your schedule is another vital aspect of effective time management. Life is dynamic, and so are your needs and interests. You can identify patterns and make necessary adjustments by assessing how you spend your time. Consider setting aside a moment each week for reflection, examining how your time has been used and what changes might enhance your routine. This practice improves efficiency and ensures your schedule remains flexible and responsive to your evolving goals. It's about finding a rhythm that suits you, allowing for spontaneity and adaptation as needed. This approach fosters a sense of empowerment as you actively shape your days to align with your desires and aspirations.

Effective time management is not about rigid schedules or constant productivity; it's about creating a life that reflects your values and passions. By prioritizing tasks, utilizing planning tools, setting boundaries, and regularly reviewing your schedule, you cultivate a routine that supports your well-being and enriches your retirement experience. Each day becomes an opportunity to fully engage with life, embracing responsibilities and joys with intention and grace.

4.4 INCORPORATING LEARNING AND PERSONAL GROWTH

In the unfolding tapestry of retirement, continuous learning emerges as a vibrant thread, weaving through days with a promise of discovery and growth. Envision the excitement of exploring new subjects, each a doorway to previously unseen worlds. Online courses have transformed this exploration, offering a wealth of knowledge at your fingertips. Whether diving into the mysteries of ancient history or unraveling the complexities of modern technology, these courses invite you to challenge your mind and expand your horizons. The flexibility of online learning means you can engage at your own pace, fitting education seamlessly into the rhythm of your life. This ongoing education isn't just about acquiring new skills; it's about nurturing a curious and agile mind that eagerly adapts to the changing world.

To make learning a joyful part of your daily routine, consider setting aside dedicated time for reading or research. Picture a cozy nook where you can escape into the pages of a gripping novel or delve into an enlightening article. This space becomes a sanctuary for your mind, inviting you to pause, reflect, and absorb. Joining groups and clubs adds a social dimension to your learning, offering opportunities to share insights and engage in stimulating discussions. These gatherings become fertile ground for new ideas and friendships, enriching your life with knowledge and connection. The act of learning transforms from a solitary pursuit to a communal experience, where shared curiosity fosters a sense of belonging and mutual support.

Setting learning goals provides direction and motivation, guiding your educational endeavors with purpose. Think of these goals as milestones on a path of personal development, each a step towards greater understanding and fulfillment. Creating a learning plan with clear objectives helps you focus your efforts, ensuring that your studies align with your interests and aspirations. This plan acts as a roadmap, highlighting the skills you wish to acquire and the subjects you would like to explore. As you achieve each milestone, take a moment to celebrate your progress, acknowledging the growth and confidence that comes from reaching your goals. These celebrations reinforce your commitment to lifelong learning, encouraging you to continue pursuing knowledge with enthusiasm and curiosity.

Curiosity is a powerful catalyst for personal growth, propelling you towards new experiences and insights. Cultivating a mindset of exploration and inquiry invites you to view the world with wonder, seeking out opportunities to learn and grow. This curiosity becomes a guiding light, illuminating paths that lead to new skills and hobbies. Encouraging experimentation opens doors to unexpected passions, transforming routine days into adventures of discovery. Whether trying your hand at painting, learning to play a musical instrument, or experimenting with new culinary creations, each hobby becomes an opportunity to expand your abilities and enrich your life. Welcome the joy of learning for its own sake, allowing your curiosity to lead you to places you've never been before.

Interactive Element: Creating Your Learning Plan

Take a moment to reflect on areas of interest you've always wanted to explore. Jot down subjects or skills that intrigue you and rank them based on your enthusiasm. Next, create a simple learning plan by setting a timeline for each subject, identifying resources, and outlining small goals. This plan serves as your guide, helping you stay focused and motivated as you embark on your educational pursuits. Periodically review and adjust your plan, celebrating each milestone you achieve along the way.

Incorporating learning and personal growth into your daily life transforms retirement into a vibrant engagement and self-discovery period. Each new subject you explore, and every skill you acquire adds depth and richness to your experience, fostering a sense of fulfillment and joy. Through learning, you remain active in the ever-evolving world, your mind is open to possibilities, and your spirit is invigorated by the thrill of discovery.

4.5 DESIGNING YOUR PERFECT DAY: A STEP-BY-STEP GUIDE

Imagine waking up to a day that unfolds precisely as you desire, where relaxation, activity, and personal fulfillment are perfectly balanced. Visualizing your ideal day can be powerful, offering a glimpse into what truly matters to you. Begin by picturing a morning that energizes you, perhaps with a peaceful walk or a cozy moment with your favorite book. Let your mind wander through the afternoon, filled with activities that spark joy—maybe a painting class or a leisurely lunch with a friend. As evening approaches, think about winding down with a serene ritual, like a warm bath, meditation, or prayer. This visualization clarifies your desires and sets the stage for turning them into reality.

Once you have a clear picture of your perfect day, it's time to translate that vision into a structured plan. Reflect on using templates for daily schedule planning to help you organize your time effectively. These templates serve as a guide, allowing you to allocate specific time slots for various activities. Incorporating a mix of activities is crucial to maintaining balance. For instance, blend physical exercise with creative pursuits, ensuring your day caters to both body and mind. This structured approach helps prevent the day from slipping away unnoticed, ensuring that each moment is purposeful and enriching.

It's essential to accept trial and error as part of designing your routine. Life is dynamic, and what works one week might need adjustment the next. Keeping a diary of daily experiences can be incredibly beneficial in refining your schedule. Note what felt satisfying and what seemed off. Did a particular task feel rushed? Was there enough time for relaxation? Use these reflections to tweak your routine, adapting to what feels right. This process is not about perfection but finding a rhythm that suits you. With each adjustment, you gain insight into what truly enhances your daily life.

Customizing your daily schedule is vital, as it ensures your routine aligns with your unique needs and preferences. Tailor your activities based on your energy levels and interests. Some of us are morning people, brimming with energy at dawn, while others find their stride in the afternoon. Recognizing these patterns allows you to schedule more demanding tasks when you feel most alert and reserve quieter activities for when your energy wanes. Personalizing your day this way boosts productivity and enhances your sense of fulfillment, as each day reflects who you are and what you value.

Designing your perfect day isn't about rigidly adhering to a plan but creating a framework supporting your goals and desires. Visualizing your ideal day, planning with intention, experimenting, and customizing your routine are all steps that guide you toward a more fulfilling and balanced life. As you explore these strategies, remember that your daily routine is a canvas, ready to be painted with the colors of your choosing, reflecting the life you aspire to lead.

4.6 EVENING REFLECTIONS: ENDING THE DAY WITH GRATITUDE

As the sun dips below the horizon, casting a warm glow over the day you've lived, take a moment to pause and reflect. Evening reflection is more than a ritual; it's a chance to acknowledge the day's experiences and cultivate a sense of gratitude. This practice can significantly enhance your well-being, as it encourages you to focus on the positives, no matter how small they may seem. Writing about positive experiences and achievements is one way to engage in this reflection. By writing down what went well, you reinforce those experiences in your mind, fostering a sense of accomplishment and contentment. Putting pen to paper transforms fleeting moments into tangible memories, allowing you to revisit them whenever you need a reminder of the good in your life.

Study incorporating mindfulness exercises that promote gratitude and appreciation to deepen your evening reflections. Writing a gratitude list before bed can be particularly effective. List three things you're thankful for—perhaps the laughter shared with a friend, the beauty of a sunset, or the satisfaction of completing a project. This practice shifts your focus from what might be lacking to what you cherish, filling your heart with warmth as you prepare for rest. Meditation or prayer can also enhance your evening routine. Imagine closing your eyes, taking slow, deliberate breaths, and allowing the day's tensions to melt away. These methods help quiet the mind, paving the way for a restful night's sleep.

Creating a peaceful bedtime routine is another essential aspect of gracefully winding down your day. Guide yourself into decompressing by establishing rituals that soothe and calm. Ponder reading a few pages of a favorite book or listening to soothing music that gently lulls you into tranquility. These activities signal to your mind and body that it's time to transition from the day's busyness to the quiet of the night. Setting a consistent bedtime further supports this transition, as it helps regulate your sleep cycle, ensuring you wake up refreshed and ready to embrace a new day. A well-established routine improves sleep quality and contributes to stability and well-being.

Reflecting on the day's events provides an opportunity for personal growth and self-awareness. As you review what transpired, consider both your accomplishments and areas where you might improve. This analysis isn't about self-criticism but about understanding and learning. What moments brought joy? What challenges did you face, and how did you respond? By examining these aspects, you gain insights into your behaviors and choices, equipping you to make more informed decisions in the future. This practice of evening reflection fosters a cycle of continuous growth, where each day's experiences build upon the last, guiding you toward a more fulfilling and mindful life.

As you explore these evening practices, remember that they are meant to enhance your routine, not complicate it. Choose activities that resonate with you and allow them to evolve as your needs change. The goal is to create a space where reflection and gratitude become natural parts of your day, setting the stage for peaceful rest and renewed energy. By ending each day with gratitude, you cultivate a mindset that appreciates life's simple joys, enriching your retirement with a sense of purpose and satisfaction.

Thus, concludes Chapter 4, inviting you to incorporate these insights into your daily life. By embracing these routines, you will create a lifestyle that balances reflection with action, rest with engagement, and solitude with connection. In the next chapter, we will explore how to build and maintain meaningful relationships, continuing to enrich this vibrant phase of life.

SHARE YOUR VOICE, INSPIRE A JOURNEY

THE GIFT OF ENCOURAGEMENT

"The best way to find yourself is to lose yourself in the service of others."

— *MAHATMA GANDHI*

Every act of generosity creates a ripple. By sharing your experience, you could brighten someone else's path.

Would you help a fellow woman ready to redefine her retirement?

My mission with *Retirement Redefined for Women* is to empower women to embrace this new chapter of life with confidence, purpose, and joy. But to reach even more women, I need your help.

Most readers pick their next book based on reviews. By leaving a review, you can help someone who might be feeling overwhelmed or uncertain find the guidance they need to create the life they dream of.

Your review could make all the difference, helping one more woman:

- Find clarity in her retirement vision.
- Build meaningful connections that enrich her life.
- Discover new passions and a renewed sense of purpose.
- Face this chapter of life with courage and confidence.

It takes less than a minute, but your thoughtful words could transform someone's journey.

To share your review and make a difference, simply scan the QR code below:

Thank you for being a part of this community and helping spread the message of empowerment and possibility. Your kindness inspires me and so many others.

With gratitude,

Victoria Spring

5

EXPLORING PURPOSEFUL ENGAGEMENT AND NEW

OPPORTUNITIES

I magine the quiet thrill of rediscovering a long-forgotten hobby, like finding a favorite book tucked away on a dusty shelf. For many women entering retirement, this chapter of life opens the door to pursuits that once brought joy but were set aside amid professional and familial commitments. Now is the perfect time to dust off those passions and explore new ones. Engaging in hobbies enriches your days and offers a therapeutic retreat from the hustle of daily life. As you delve into these pursuits, you'll find they can bring a profound sense of fulfillment and serenity.

Hobbies have a remarkable way of lifting spirits and alleviating stress. Examine the calming nature of painting, where each brushstroke becomes a meditative practice. The canvas offers a space to express emotions, transforming them into vibrant colors and shapes. Similarly, pottery invites you to mold and shape with your hands, grounding you in the present moment. These creative outlets serve as a form of mindfulness, allowing you to focus entirely on the task at hand. Such activities have been shown to reduce stress and anxiety, promoting mental well-being. Gardening, too, provides a therapeutic escape, connecting you with nature's rhythm. Digging in the soil, tending to plants, and watching them flourish can be a source of deep satisfaction and joy.

Reintegrating hobbies into your daily routine doesn't have to be overwhelming. The key is to set aside dedicated time each week for these activities. Give thought to blocking off an hour every Tuesday afternoon for your artistic endeavors or reserving Saturday mornings for tending your garden. By carving out this time, you create a ritual that becomes a cherished part of your routine. This consistency nurtures your interests and ensures that hobbies remain a priority amid life's demands. Over time, these moments become something to look forward to, a sanctuary where you can recharge and explore your creative side.

The social dimensions of hobbies should not be underestimated. Engaging in activities alongside others offers opportunities to meet like-minded individuals and build new friendships. Local clubs and community workshops serve as gathering places for those who share your passions. Whether it's a knitting circle that meets weekly or a photography group that organizes monthly outings, these settings foster connections that enrich your social life. Participating in classes or workshops provides a supportive environment to learn and grow. Here, you can exchange ideas, share techniques, and celebrate each other's progress. These interactions enhance the joy of hobbies, turning solitary pursuits into shared experiences.

Interactive Element: Hobby Exploration Checklist

Take a moment to reflect on hobbies that pique your interest or those you've always wanted to try. Create a checklist that includes these activities along with local clubs, workshops, or classes that offer them. Explore community centers or online resources to find opportunities that align with your interests. This checklist can guide you in planning your engagement with hobbies, ensuring they become an integral and enjoyable part of your retirement.

As you explore these hobbies, you may be drawn to new interests you hadn't considered before. The beauty of this stage in life is the freedom to experiment, to try something new without the pressure of perfection. Whether you choose to paint landscapes, tend a garden, or join a club, let these activities be a source of joy and fulfillment. Pursuing hobbies is a journey of discovery, one that invites you to engage with life in deeply rewarding ways.

5.1 LIFELONG LEARNING: EMBRACING EDUCATION AT ANY AGE

Picture yourself seated at your dining room table with a glass of iced tea as you dive into an online course. The world of lifelong learning is at your fingertips, offering boundless opportunities to expand your horizons. This stage of life, often seen as a time to slow down, can instead become a period of enrichment and growth. By embracing continuous education, you unlock personal development and fulfillment pathways that keep your mind agile and engaged. Visualize enrolling in courses from platforms like Coursera or Udemy, where you can explore everything from creative writing to data science. These platforms provide the flexibility to learn at your own pace, allowing you to delve into subjects that have always intrigued you. Whether you're deepening a long held passion or venturing into new territories, the joy of learning lies in the discovery itself.

For those who prefer a more structured environment, local community colleges and adult education programs offer a wealth of resources. These institutions are treasure troves of knowledge waiting to be explored. Community colleges often provide courses tailored for retirees, making it easier to connect with peers who share your interests. Adult education classes cover a wide range of subjects, from languages to arts to technology, ensuring there's something for everyone. By attending these classes, you acquire new skills and become part of a community of learners, enriching your social life in unexpected ways. The camaraderie in these settings can be as rewarding as the knowledge gained, fostering friendships that enhance your educational experience.

The cognitive benefits of lifelong learning extend beyond the acquisition of new skills. Engaging in continuous education keeps your mind active and sharp, staving off cognitive decline associated with aging. Think about studying a new language using apps like Duolingo, making language learning accessible and enjoyable. These apps offer bite-sized lessons that fit seamlessly into your daily routine, turning spare moments into opportunities for growth. Engaging in puzzles and logic games further stimulates your brain, challenging you to think critically and solve problems. These activities provide mental exercise and instill a sense of accomplishment, boosting your confidence and sense of agency. You create a fusion of intellectual engagement that enriches your life with learning that enhancing your days.

Setting educational goals is a powerful way to focus your efforts and track your progress. These goals are steppingstones, guiding you toward your broader aspirations. Begin by identifying areas you wish to explore, then create a personalized learning plan with clear milestones. This plan serves as a roadmap, helping you stay organized and motivated. Whether you aim to complete a specific course, master a new skill, or indulge your curiosity, having defined objectives provides direction and purpose. Tracking your progress along the way allows you to celebrate achievements, no matter how small, reinforcing the joy of learning. By maintaining a sense of curiosity and openness, you invite endless opportunities for discovery and growth into your life.

5.2 ENCORE CAREERS: TURNING PASSION INTO PURPOSE

Imagine stepping into a role that aligns with your deepest passions and brings a profound sense of fulfillment. Encore careers offer this unique opportunity, allowing you to pursue work that resonates with your values and interests, even after stepping away from your primary career. These roles can take many forms, from consulting to teaching, and often provide a chance to leverage years of experience in new and meaningful ways. For instance, if you've spent decades in corporate management, you might find joy in mentoring young entrepreneurs or leading workshops that teach business fundamentals. Teaching, whether in a local community college or through online platforms, can also be an enriching avenue, allowing you to impart knowledge while staying engaged with a subject you love. The beauty of an encore career lies in its flexibility and purpose, enabling you to shape this new chapter of life around what truly matters to you.

Identifying a potential encore career begins with introspection. Reflect on your skills, interests, and what brings you joy. Study what aspects of your previous work you found most rewarding and how they might translate into a new career. Self-assessment exercises can be invaluable, helping you uncover strengths and passions you may not have fully recognized. For example, jot down your professional accomplishments and interests, then look for patterns or connections to guide your encore career choice.

Perhaps you've always had a knack for organizing events or a passion for writing. These insights can point you toward opportunities that align with your talents and desires, setting the stage for a fulfilling and purpose-driven career.

Pursuing an encore career offers numerous benefits that extend beyond financial stability. These roles can provide a renewed sense of purpose, helping you stay mentally and socially engaged. They also open doors to mentorship and leadership opportunities within your chosen field, allowing you to guide and support others while continuing your own professional growth. Envision the satisfaction of mentoring a group of aspiring professionals or leading a community project that makes a tangible difference. These experiences enrich your life and positively impact those around you. Furthermore, an encore career can bridge retirement and full-time work, offering the flexibility to balance work with leisure and other interests.

Transitioning into an encore career requires careful planning and a proactive approach. Start by building connections in your desired field through networking. Attend industry events, join professional associations, and engage with online communities to meet others who share your interests. Networking introduces you to potential opportunities and provides insights and advice from those already established in the field. Online resources can also be instrumental in facilitating career transitions. Websites like LinkedIn offer tools for career exploration and skill development. At the same time, platforms such as Coursera provide courses that can help you update or acquire new skills relevant to your chosen path. By leveraging these resources, you can equip yourself with the knowledge and connections needed to succeed in your encore career.

5.3 VOLUNTEERING WITH IMPACT: FINDING THE RIGHT FIT

Imagine finding a role that fills your days with purpose and leaves an indelible mark on the community around you. Purposeful volunteering provides this opportunity, bridging the gap between personal growth and community betterment. Choosing roles that resonate with your passions and skills allows you to contribute meaningfully while enriching your life. In local nonprofits, roles vary from mentoring young students in literacy programs to organizing events for community outreach. These positions provide a platform to apply your unique talents in ways that make a tangible difference. Engaging in such roles supports vital community needs and fosters a profound sense of fulfillment and accomplishment, inviting you to become an integral part of the community's fabric.

To find the right volunteering opportunity, consider what you enjoy and where your strengths lie. Reflect on past experiences that brought you joy or a sense of achievement. Perhaps you thrived in leadership roles or found satisfaction in creative endeavors. Once you have a clearer picture, explore volunteering databases like Volunteer Match or Idealist. These platforms act as bridges, connecting you with causes that align with your interests. Whether it's working with animals, supporting environmental initiatives, or helping in educational settings, these resources simplify the process of finding the perfect fit. By specifying your preferences and skills, you're more likely to find an opportunity that feels rewarding and genuinely engaging. This approach ensures that your volunteer work benefits others and enhances your sense of purpose and satisfaction.

The benefits of volunteering extend beyond the immediate impact of your efforts. It creates an environment where personal fulfillment and community support go hand in hand. As you work alongside fellow volunteers, you forge relationships built on shared goals and camaraderie. These connections often blossom into friendships, providing a social network that enriches your life. Furthermore, volunteering allows you to gain new skills and insights, broadening your horizons and enhancing your adaptability. Whether learning event planning, developing communication skills, or acquiring practical knowledge in a new field, these experiences contribute to your personal growth. They equip you with valuable tools in volunteer settings that are applicable to various aspects of life. Through volunteering, you engage in a continuous cycle of learning and giving, each reinforcing the other.

Consistency is key to making a lasting impact through volunteer work. Regular involvement allows you to build deeper relationships within the organization and community, making your contributions more meaningful. Consider setting a volunteer schedule that suits your lifestyle, whether weekly, bi-weekly, or monthly commitments. This regularity benefits the organization by providing reliable support and seamlessly integrating volunteering into your routine. By committing to a consistent schedule, you reinforce your role as a dependable and valued member of the team. Over time, this commitment leads to more significant projects and responsibilities, amplifying your impact and deepening your connection to the cause. Regular volunteering becomes a rhythm that adds structure and purpose to your days, enriching your life and those you touch.

5.4 TRAVELING WITH A PURPOSE: COMBINING LEISURE AND SERVICE

Picture stepping off a plane in a new country, your senses alive with the colors, sounds, and scents of a place waiting to be explored. But this isn't just any trip—it's one where you combine leisure with meaningful service, creating a medley of experiences that enrich your life and those you meet. This is purposeful travel, a chance to immerse yourself in different cultures while contributing to the local community. Programs like Habitat for Humanity offer such opportunities, where you can help build homes and hope, connecting with people in ways that ordinary tourism often doesn't allow.

The appeal of purposeful travel lies in its ability to transform a vacation into a deeply enriching experience. Visualize spending a week in a small village, working alongside locals on community projects. You learn about their traditions, share meals, and engage in conversations that deepen your understanding of the world. This kind of travel fosters a genuine cultural exchange, breaking down barriers and building bridges. It allows you to step outside your comfort zone, embracing the unknown with curiosity and openness. Through these interactions, you gain insights that challenge preconceived notions, fostering empathy and broadening your worldview. Such experiences are transformative and leave a lasting impact on the communities you assist, creating memories that linger long after you've returned home.

Planning a purposeful trip requires some research and organization. Begin by exploring organizations like Global Volunteers, which offer structured programs designed to match your skills and interests with community needs. These organizations provide the framework and support necessary to ensure your efforts are practical and appreciated. They often handle logistics such as accommodation and meals, allowing you to focus on the work and the experience. Think about your abilities and what you hope to gain from the trip, then choose a program that aligns with these goals. Whether you're drawn to teaching English, participating in environmental conservation, or assisting in healthcare initiatives, there's a project that can benefit from your enthusiasm and expertise. These opportunities allow you to engage with the world in meaningful ways, enriching your travel experiences beyond what sightseeing alone can offer.

As you embark on these journeys, it's valuable to document your experiences, capturing the moments that resonate deeply with you. Keeping a travel log can be a powerful tool for reflection, helping you process and appreciate the impact of your trip. Write about the people you meet, the challenges you face, and the lessons you learn. These reflections enhance your personal growth and serve as a record of your contributions and the change you've witnessed. Photos and sketches can complement your words, adding a visual dimension to your memories. Upon returning home, revisiting these entries can provide clarity and perspective, reinforcing the personal growth and cultural understanding gained through your travels. Sharing your stories with friends and family can also inspire others to contemplate purposeful travel, spreading the message of global citizenship and service.

Purposeful travel invites you to see the world through a different lens, where every interaction holds the potential for learning and connection. It challenges you to engage with communities in a way that respects and honors their traditions while contributing positively to their development. This kind of travel offers a chance to give back, creating a ripple effect of goodwill and understanding that extends far beyond the boundaries of the trip itself. As you plan your next adventure, consider how you might incorporate service into your itinerary, transforming your travels into an enriching experience that benefits you and the world around you.

5.5 MENTORING: SHARING WISDOM AND BUILDING LEGACY

Imagine the profound impact of sharing your life's wisdom with someone eager to learn and grow. Mentoring offers this invaluable opportunity, allowing you to impart your knowledge and experiences to younger generations. In doing so, you help shape their futures while creating a legacy beyond your immediate circle. Programs within local schools or community centers provide structured avenues to engage in mentoring, offering a platform to guide and inspire. Whether it's mentoring a young student struggling with math or advising an aspiring entrepreneur on business strategies, these relationships have the power to transform lives. By sharing your journey, you enrich others and reinforce the value of your experiences.

To become an effective mentor, it's essential to cultivate specific skills that foster open and meaningful relationships. Active listening is at the heart of any successful mentoring relationship. It involves giving full attention, acknowledging feelings, and responding thoughtfully. This creates a safe space where mentees feel heard and valued, encouraging them to share their thoughts and challenges. Strong communication skills are equally important, ensuring that advice is conveyed clearly and constructively. By practicing empathy and patience, you can guide mentees through their difficulties, helping them find solutions and build confidence. These interactions also offer opportunities for personal growth as you learn from your mentees' perspectives and experiences.

The rewards of mentoring extend far beyond the satisfaction of helping others. Such relationships often foster a sense of achievement and fulfillment that enriches your life. Consider the pride in seeing your mentee succeed, knowing that your guidance played a role in their journey. These stories of successful mentoring relationships illustrate the profound impact that mentorship can have. Give thought to the case of a retired teacher who mentored a high school student, helping them gain confidence and improve their academic performance. This success benefited the student and gave the mentor a renewed sense of purpose and connection. As a mentor, you gain as much as you give, discovering new insights and rejuvenating your own enthusiasm for learning and growth.

Participating in formal mentoring programs can enhance your mentoring experience, providing support and resources to help you succeed. Local and online mentoring networks connect you with individuals seeking guidance in various fields. These programs often offer training sessions, workshops, and resources to help you develop your mentoring skills. By joining such initiatives, you become part of a community of mentors who share your commitment to making a difference. The possibilities are vast and varied, whether you choose a program focused on education, business, or personal development. Engaging in these networks expands your reach and enriches your mentoring experience with diverse perspectives and ideas.

As you consider the role of mentoring in your life, remember that it is a dynamic and evolving process. Each interaction offers the chance to learn and grow, both for you and your mentee. Through mentoring, you create a lasting legacy that touches lives and inspires future generations. Your wisdom becomes a guiding light, illuminating paths and opening doors for those who follow. In sharing your knowledge, you ensure that your impact endures, resonating long after your mentoring journey has concluded. This chapter on purposeful engagement and new opportunities underscores the myriad ways to enrich your life in retirement, from hobbies to mentoring. As you welcome these opportunities, you'll find that they enhance your days, filling them with meaningful interactions and lifelong learning.

6

NAVIGATING FAMILY DYNAMICS AND RELATIONSHIPS

Imagine a Sunday afternoon at your home, the air filled with the aroma of freshly brewed coffee. Your daughter stops by with her kids, and suddenly, your quiet retreat transforms into a lively gathering. While these moments bring joy, they also highlight the need to balance family interactions with personal time. As women, we often wear many hats—caretaker, mediator, confidante—which is even more pronounced as we transition into retirement. The challenge lies in setting boundaries that honor our needs and our families. This chapter invites you to explore the art of boundary-setting to maintain harmony and personal wellbeing.

6.1 SETTING BOUNDARIES: BALANCING FAMILY NEEDS AND PERSONAL TIME

Setting boundaries can sometimes feel elusive, yet it is essential for maintaining healthy relationships and preserving our sense of self. Visualize boundaries as invisible lines that define where your responsibilities end, and others begin. These lines protect your time, energy, and emotional resources, ensuring you can nurture yourself while being present for your family. Clear boundaries help manage expectations, allowing family members to understand your limits and respect your space. They prevent overextension and resentment, creating a foundation for mutual respect and understanding.

Assertive communication is key to establishing these boundaries effectively. It involves expressing your needs clearly and confidently, without anger or guilt. Techniques like using "I" statements can be helpful. For example, saying, "I need some quiet time in the afternoons to recharge," communicates your needs without placing blame. Creating a family calendar can also be a practical tool to allocate time for personal and family activities. By visibly scheduling commitments and downtime, you set expectations and reduce the chances of overbooking. This visual representation is a gentle reminder to you and your family to honor the time set aside for yourself.

Maintaining boundaries requires strategies that uphold your decisions without guilt or discomfort. One approach is to practice saying no gracefully. It's okay to decline requests that encroach on your personal time. Phrases like, "I appreciate the invitation, but I need some time to myself," can convey your decision kindly yet firmly. It's important to remember that saying no to others often means saying yes to yourself, opening up space for activities that rejuvenate you. Upholding boundaries might feel challenging initially, but over time, it becomes a liberating practice that empowers you to lead a balanced life.

Open dialogue about needs and limits is crucial in fostering understanding and cooperation within your family. Regular family meetings provide a platform to discuss boundaries and adjust them as necessary. During these meetings, encourage each member to express their needs and listen actively to others. This open communication nurtures empathy and creates an environment where everyone's boundaries are respected. It also offers an opportunity to address any concerns or conflicts that may arise, ensuring that solutions are collaborative and considerate.

Examine common scenarios where setting boundaries is necessary, such as handling requests for childcare or errands. While it can be rewarding to support your family, it's essential to be mindful of your capacity. If a family member frequently asks for help, you might say, "I'm happy to assist occasionally, but I also need time for my own activities." This statement acknowledges your willingness to help while clearly defining your limits. By setting these boundaries, you preserve your energy and maintain balance in your life.

Interactive Element: Boundary-Setting Reflection

Reflect on a recent instance when you felt your personal boundaries were being encroached upon. Consider your reaction to this situation and how alternative communication might have protected your boundaries better. Jot down some "I" statements or alternative responses that would have more clearly expressed your needs. This reflective exercise is designed to enhance your assertive communication skills, equipping you for future situations that may require firm boundary-setting.

Navigating family dynamics in retirement offers challenges and opportunities for growth. By setting and maintaining clear boundaries, you create a harmonious environment that respects your and your family's needs, allowing you to enjoy your relationships while nurturing your well-being.

6.2 PARTNERING IN RETIREMENT: STRENGTHENING MARITAL BONDS

Retirement brings a significant shift in marital dynamics, transforming the daily rhythm couples have known for years. With career obligations behind you, the time spent together often increases, necessitating adjustments in how roles are shared. This phase can be rewarding and challenging, as it invites reevaluating household responsibilities. Picture a typical day where both of you share chores with ease, whether it's preparing meals or organizing the home. This mutual participation fosters a sense of equality and partnership, creating a balanced environment where both partners feel valued and supported. By sharing these tasks, you lighten the load and cultivate a deeper connection through teamwork and cooperation.

Beyond the practicalities of daily life, retirement offers a unique opportunity to strengthen the intimacy and connection that underpin a lasting marriage. Planning regular date nights or joint activities can rekindle the spark, reminding you of the joy found in each other's company. Whether it's a cozy dinner at home, a walk in the park, or a weekend getaway, these shared experiences build memories that enrich your bond. Additionally, practicing active listening and empathy provides a foundation for understanding and closeness. This involves truly hearing each other, acknowledging feelings, and responding with compassion. Creating a safe space for open dialogue nurtures a relationship where both partners feel heard and cherished.

Shared goals and activities are vital in enhancing marital satisfaction during retirement. Pursuing common interests fosters a sense of purpose and unity, turning shared dreams into reality. Think about taking up a new hobby together, such as gardening, painting, or learning a musical instrument. These ventures offer opportunities to grow and discover new aspects of each other, keeping your relationship vibrant and dynamic. Planning travel adventures can also bring excitement and anticipation as you explore new destinations and cultures. These shared endeavors strengthen your bond and create a melting pot of experiences that enrich your lives.

Resolving conflicts constructively is crucial for maintaining harmony, especially when spending more time together. Effective communication is key and using "I" statements can be a powerful tool. For example, expressing, "I feel overwhelmed when the house is cluttered," rather than assigning blame, opens the door for collaboration and problem-solving. This approach encourages both partners to take responsibility for their feelings and actions, fostering a sense of partnership in addressing issues. It's about finding solutions that respect both perspectives, ensuring that disagreements become opportunities for growth rather than sources of tension. By addressing conflicts with kindness and understanding, you create a resilient and harmonious relationship that thrives in the face of change.

Retirement is a chapter that invites reflection and renewal, offering couples the chance to deepen their connection and envision new possibilities. By adopting these strategies, you can navigate the shifts in marital dynamics with grace and joy, ensuring that your partnership remains a source of strength and fulfillment. The journey may require adjustments, but with open hearts and minds, it promises to be a rewarding experience.

6.3 GRANDPARENTING: JOYS AND CHALLENGES IN A NEW ROLE

The role of grandparenting often arrives with a wave of joy, introducing new dimensions to family life. Grandchildren's laughter fills your home, creating a warm, lively, invigorating, and comforting atmosphere. There's a unique kind of fulfillment in this stage, where you can engage with your grandchildren without the pressures of being a parent. You have the opportunity to create memorable traditions, such as baking cookies every Sunday or embarking on nature walks to discover the wonders of the outdoors together. These activities foster deep bonds and pass down values and stories that shape the young ones' understanding of their heritage and identity.

Yet, grandparenting is not without its challenges. Balancing your involvement with personal time can be a delicate act, especially when you cherish your newfound freedom in retirement. The excitement of spending time with grandchildren can sometimes lead to overcommitment, leaving you stretched thin. Managing expectations becomes crucial, as family members may assume your availability for babysitting or other tasks. It's essential to clearly communicate your limits, ensuring your time and energy are protected. This balance allows you to enjoy precious moments with your grandchildren while maintaining the space you need for yourself.

Building strong relationships with your grandchildren involves more than just spending time together; it requires intentional interaction. Sharing family stories or history can be an enriching experience, offering children a sense of belonging and continuity. These tales become a bridge between generations, connecting your past with their present. Engaging in educational or creative activities, such as crafting or reading together, can also strengthen these bonds. These shared experiences nurture curiosity, learning, and create a reservoir of cherished memories they will carry into adulthood.

As a grandparent, setting boundaries around your personal space while enjoying your role is essential for maintaining balance. Establishing regular visitation schedules can help manage your needs and those of your family. This approach ensures that you can plan activities around your commitments while still being an integral part of your grandchildren's lives. It's about finding the sweet spot where you can be present and supportive without feeling overwhelmed. By setting these parameters, you create a healthy dynamic that respects your autonomy and fosters a nurturing environment for your grandchildren.

Grandparenting is a journey filled with love, laughter, and growth. It offers you the chance to impact your grandchildren's lives positively while continuing to learn and adapt. Welcome this role with an open heart, allowing yourself the freedom to explore the joys and navigate the challenges with confidence and grace.

6.4 THE SANDWICH GENERATION: CARING FOR PARENTS AND CHILDREN

Suppose you're juggling a conference call while preparing dinner, and just as you're about to catch a breath, your phone buzzes with a message from your mom about her latest medical appointment. This scene encapsulates the life of many in the sandwich generation, caught between the needs of aging parents and adult children. It's a delicate balance, requiring emotional resilience and logistical prowess. Caring for elderly parents often involves coordinating care plans, managing medications, and attending numerous appointments. It's a role that demands patience, compassion, and the ability to navigate healthcare systems and advocate for your parent's needs. At the same time, your adult children may need support, whether a listening ear or help with their parenting challenges. Balancing these dual responsibilities can feel overwhelming, as each day presents a new set of priorities and demands.

To manage these caregiving roles effectively, setting clear priorities is crucial. Begin by identifying which duties are most urgent and which can wait. This might mean addressing a parent's immediate health concern before helping a child with a routine matter. Once priorities are established, review delegating tasks when possible. Enlist the help of siblings or other family members to share the load. If you're managing a parent's medical appointments, perhaps a sibling can assist with grocery shopping or household chores. Community resources and support groups can also provide assistance and relief. Many organizations offer caregiver support programs, providing respite care and counseling services. These resources can be invaluable, offering a network of support and expertise to help you navigate the complexities of caregiving.

Amid these responsibilities, it's vital to prioritize your own wellbeing. As caregivers, we often place our needs last, but neglecting self-care can lead to burnout and fatigue. Schedule regular activities that rejuvenate you, whether a brisk walk, a yoga class, or simply reading a book. These moments of self-care are not selfish —they're necessary for maintaining your physical and mental health. Taking care of yourself ensures you have the energy and resilience to support your family effectively. Remember, you can't pour from an empty cup, so make self-care a non-negotiable part of your routine.

Effective communication is key to managing caregiving roles and responsibilities. Family meetings provide a platform to discuss duties and share updates on your parent's health and well-being. During these gatherings, encourage open dialogue to ensure everyone is on the same page. Discuss the challenges you're facing and explore solutions collaboratively. By working together, family members can devise a plan that distributes tasks equitably and respects each person's capacity. If tensions arise, approach them with empathy and a willingness to understand different perspectives. By fostering an environment of cooperation and understanding, you create a support system that benefits everyone involved.

Caring for parents and children is no small feat, but with the right strategies and support, it can be a fulfilling aspect of your life. Accept this role with compassion and determination, knowing that your efforts make a significant difference in the lives of those you love. As you navigate the challenges of the sandwich generation, take pride in the strength and resilience you demonstrate each day.

6.5 COMMUNICATING EFFECTIVELY WITH FAMILY MEMBERS

We all know that communication is the glue that holds a family together. It's not just about exchanging words; it's about fostering understanding and cooperation among the people we love. Envision trying to assemble a puzzle without all the pieces fitting together—communication fills those gaps. Practicing active listening is one way to enhance this vital skill. When we truly listen, we give our full attention to the person speaking, setting aside distractions and judgments. This simple act can transform interactions, making others feel valued and understood. In a world full of noise, being genuinely heard is a gift.

Improving communication within the family involves more than just listening; it requires clarity and simplicity in how we express ourselves. Using clear and concise language avoids misunderstandings and minimizes assumptions. Think of it as painting with bold strokes instead of intricate details—direct yet gentle. Also, encouraging open-ended questions invites dialogue and exploration rather than shutting down conversations. Questions like, "What do you think about this idea?" or "How do you feel about the changes happening?" open the floor for discussions, inviting everyone to share their thoughts and feelings openly. This approach enriches conversations and strengthens bonds by promoting understanding.

Family conflicts are inevitable, but how we handle them can make all the difference. Conflict resolution techniques offer pathways to peaceful outcomes, turning disagreements into opportunities for growth. Consider mediation or facilitated family discussions as tools to navigate these challenging waters. These structured conversations provide a safe space for everyone to voice their concerns, fostering an environment of mutual respect. By focusing on solutions rather than blame, families can work collaboratively to resolve issues. This process involves acknowledging each person's perspective, validating their feelings, and seeking common ground. It's about building bridges, not walls, and finding ways to move forward together.

Regular family check-ins are an excellent way to address concerns and share updates, ensuring everyone remains connected and informed. Setting aside time for weekly or monthly family meetings creates a routine that supports open communication and transparency. These gatherings offer a platform to discuss any changes, challenges, or achievements, keeping everyone on the same page. By maintaining this rhythm of communication, families can prevent misunderstandings and strengthen their connections. It's also an opportunity to celebrate successes, no matter how small, fostering a sense of unity and shared purpose.

In the tapestry of family life, communication is the thread that weaves through every interaction, binding us together in a shared narrative. By embracing these techniques and practices, you can cultivate a family environment that thrives on understanding, compassion, and cooperation. Effective communication empowers each member to express themselves authentically, enriching relationships and creating a harmonious home.

6.6 INVOLVING FAMILY IN YOUR RETIREMENT JOURNEY

Retirement, a time often marked by personal reflection and new beginnings, can also offer an excellent opportunity to strengthen your family ties. Sharing your retirement goals with your family is more than just a conversation—it's an invitation for them to understand and support you as you transition into this new phase of life. By discussing your financial plans, you provide clarity and foster a sense of inclusion, ensuring everyone is on the same page. Imagine sitting with your loved ones around the dining table, openly sharing your aspirations, whether it's downsizing to a cozy home or embarking on that long-dreamed-of cross-country road trip. These discussions build mutual understanding and allow family members to offer their insights and perhaps even join you in some of your adventures. When family members know your plans, they can become allies in helping you achieve them, offering advice or assistance where needed, and celebrating milestones as they occur.

Involving your family in retirement experiences can deepen these connections. Contemplate inviting them to participate in volunteer projects that align with your values and interests. Whether it's planting trees in a local park or helping at the community food bank, these shared activities foster a sense of purpose and strengthen familial bonds. Volunteering together enriches your retirement and sets an example of service and community engagement for younger family members. Hosting family events or gatherings also provides a chance to connect. From casual backyard barbecues to more structured family reunions, these occasions allow you to share your retirement journey in a quiet setting. Such gatherings provide a platform for storytelling, laughter, and the creation of new memories, reinforcing the ties that bind your family together.

Managing family expectations is crucial to maintaining harmony during your retirement. Setting realistic boundaries and roles within joint activities or projects is important. For instance, if you're spearheading a family reunion, clearly define who will handle logistics, manage invitations, and coordinate activities. This clarity prevents misunderstandings and ensures that everyone feels valued and involved. Family members are more likely to embrace their responsibilities and contribute positively when roles are well-defined. Setting these expectations from the outset creates a collaborative environment where everyone knows their part and works together toward a common goal.

Celebrating milestones with your family can bring immense joy and a sense of accomplishment. Whether it's your retirement anniversary or the completion of a significant personal project, these moments are worth acknowledging. Planning joint celebrations for such achievements allows you to share your triumphs with those you love. You might host a dinner to toast a year of retirement or organize a small gathering to unveil a creative project you've completed. These celebrations highlight your successes and provide an opportunity for your family to express their pride and support. They reinforce the idea that retirement is a vibrant time of life, filled with achievements and new adventures, and that your family is an integral part of that journey.

Through these shared experiences, you create a rich medley of family connections that enhance your retirement. Involving your family in your plans, activities, and celebrations fosters a supportive and collaborative environment that enriches your life and theirs. As you move forward, these bonds will continue to grow, offering comfort, joy, and a sense of belonging. Retirement becomes not just an individual experience, but a shared one filled with love, laughter, and lasting memories.

7

MAINTAINING PHYSICAL AND MENTAL WELLNESS

Visualize standing at the edge of a serene lake, early morning mist swirling around you, the air crisp and invigorating. This scene embodies the essence of retirement—a time to refresh and renew, to welcome the vitality that comes from nurturing body and mind. In this stage of life, maintaining physical and mental wellness becomes not just a goal but a necessity for a vibrant and fulfilling existence. As we explore ways to stay active, remember that each movement you make is a step towards longevity and enhanced quality of life.

7.1 STAYING ACTIVE: EXERCISE ROUTINES FOR EVERY LEVEL

Regular physical activity is your ally in the quest for a long, healthy life. Exercise is more than just movement; it's a powerful tool that supports cardiovascular health, strengthens bones, and boosts mood. Engaging in regular exercise can reduce the risk of chronic illnesses, such as heart disease and diabetes, and enhance cognitive function, giving you the energy and mental clarity to savor each

day fully. The benefits extend beyond the physical, as exercise also acts as a balm for the psyche, releasing endorphins that uplift the spirit and foster a sense of achievement.

Incorporating a variety of exercise routines into your life can cater to different fitness levels and preferences, ensuring that staying active remains enjoyable and sustainable. For those seeking gentle pursuit, low-impact exercises like walking and swimming offer an ideal starting point. Walking, a simple yet effective exercise, strengthens muscles and lowers the risk of several diseases. On the other hand, swimming provides a full body workout, engaging multiple muscle groups without placing undue stress on the joints. These activities can be easily adapted to your pace, gradually allowing you to build endurance and strength.

Strength training, an often-overlooked aspect of fitness, plays a crucial role in maintaining muscle mass and bone density as we age. Incorporating exercises like light weightlifting or resistance band workouts can help preserve physical functionality, enabling you to perform daily tasks with ease and confidence. These routines can be tailored to suit your comfort level, gradually increasing intensity as your strength improves. Strength training sessions can be done at home with minimal equipment, making them accessible and convenient.

To make physical activity a seamless part of daily life, give thought to integrating movement into routine tasks. Household chores, such as gardening or cleaning, can double as exercise, providing a practical way to stay active without dedicating extra time. Gardening, in particular, offers a unique combination of physical exertion and mental relaxation. Planting, weeding, and harvesting burn calories and foster a connection with nature, providing a sense of peace and accomplishment. These activities transform mundane tasks into opportunities for movement, keeping you engaged and active throughout the day.

Participating in group exercise classes or local walking clubs can provide additional motivation and enjoyment. The social aspect of group activities creates a supportive environment, encouraging you to push beyond perceived limits while fostering camaraderie and friendship. Joining a dance class or community yoga group offers a chance to learn new skills and meet like-minded individuals, enhancing physical and emotional well-being. These gatherings provide a sense of belonging and shared purpose, reminding you that the journey to wellness is one best traveled together.

Interactive Element: Craft Your Fitness Schedule

Take a moment to design a weekly fitness schedule that incorporates a mix of exercises you enjoy. Include at least two low-impact activities like walking or swimming sessions and add strength training exercises twice a week. Contemplate joining a local group class for social interaction. Track your progress over the next month, noting how you feel physically and mentally. This schedule serves as a guide to ensure that physical activity remains a consistent and rewarding part of your routine.

7.2 NUTRITION AND WELLNESS: EATING FOR LONGEVITY

Envision a kitchen bathed in sunlight, brimming with the vibrant colors of fresh fruits and vegetables. Every color signifies the variety of nutrients within, each serving as a cornerstone for sustained health and longevity. The role of nutrition is fundamental, underpinning our physical and mental well-being. A balanced diet lays the groundwork for optimal health, fueling our bodies to

| RETIREMENT REDEFINED FOR WOMEN

function at their peak. Eating goes beyond mere satiety; it involves enriching our bodies with a diverse array of nutrients that collectively bolster our health.

Consuming a wide range of nutrients is crucial. Think of your diet as a mosaic, each piece representing a different group: carbohydrates, fats, proteins, vitamins, and minerals. Together, they form a complete picture of health. Including a variety of fruits and vegetables in your meals ensures you receive an array of vitamins and antioxidants, which help fend off illness and keep you feeling vibrant. Lean proteins, like chicken, fish, and legumes, play a vital role in repairing tissues and building muscle, while whole grains provide sustained energy and support heart health. This balance helps maintain a healthy weight, reducing the risk of chronic diseases that can diminish your quality of life.

Guidelines for a balanced diet are simple yet impactful. Aim to fill half your plate with fruits and vegetables at each meal. This practice adds color and flavor to your dishes but also boosts your intake of essential nutrients. Incorporate lean proteins and whole grains into your meals, focusing on portion sizes that satisfy without overindulging. These foods support your body's needs, providing the energy required for daily activities and the nutrients necessary for overall health. By being mindful of what you eat, you set the stage for a vibrant lifestyle that supports your goals and aspirations.

Mindful eating transforms meals from a routine task into a meaningful experience. It encourages you to savor each bite, paying attention to flavors, textures, and aromas. This practice helps you recognize hunger cues, allowing you to eat in response to your body's needs rather than external triggers. Begin by taking a moment to appreciate your food before you eat. Chew slowly, noticing the taste and texture of each mouthful. This awareness enhances enjoyment but also aids digestion and prevents overeating. By cultivating a mindful approach to eating, you create a positive relationship with food that nourishes body and mind.

Hydration is a foundation of health, yet it's often overlooked. Water is essential for every cell and function in your body, from regulating temperature to transporting nutrients. Aim to drink at least eight glasses of water daily, more if you're active or in a hot climate. Listen to your body; thirst is a clear signal that you need to hydrate, but don't wait until you're parched to take a sip. Signs of dehydration can include fatigue, dizziness, and dry skin. Keeping a water bottle nearby can serve as a reminder to drink regularly throughout the day, ensuring your body remains well hydrated and ready to tackle whatever comes your way.

7.3 MINDFULNESS AND MEDITATION: TOOLS FOR EMOTIONAL HEALTH

Picture settling into a comfy chair as the day's chaos gently fades away, replaced by a soothing sense of tranquility. This is the power of mindfulness and meditation, practices nurturing emotional well-being for centuries. In our fast-paced lives, these simple yet profound techniques offer a refuge—a way to center ourselves in the present moment. Practicing mindfulness means paying attention to the here and now and observing your thoughts and feelings without judgment. This awareness helps reduce anxiety and stress, creating a space where peace can flourish. Meditation, a close companion to mindfulness, deepens this experience by focusing your mind, often through a specific technique or mantra. Together, they form a powerful duo, fostering resilience and emotional balance.

Bringing meditation into your daily routine doesn't require hours of dedication or a unique setting. Start with brief guided breathing exercises, which can be done anywhere, anytime. Find a comfortable spot, close your eyes, and take a deep breath in through your nose, letting your chest and abdomen expand. Hold it for a moment, then exhale slowly through your mouth. Repeat this process, allowing each breath to wash away tension and invite tranquility. This simple practice quiets your body and quiets your mind, bringing clarity and focus to your day. Another effective technique is the body scan meditation, which promotes awareness by focusing on different parts of your body in sequence. Begin at your toes and gradually move upward, pausing to notice any sensations or tension. This practice helps ground you in the present, fostering a deeper connection between mind and body.

Establishing a regular meditation routine can be a transformative commitment to your well-being. Designate a specific time each day for your practice, whether it's a few peaceful minutes in the morning or a calming session before bed. Creating a dedicated space for meditation, free from distractions, enhances the experience. This could be a quiet place in your home where you can retreat, surrounded by objects that bring you peace, such as a soft cushion or a gentle candle. Consistency is key; even a short, daily practice can yield significant benefits over time. As you cultivate this habit, your ability to manage stress and navigate life's challenges strengthens, bringing a newfound sense of balance and contentment.

The accessibility of mindfulness resources makes it easier than ever to integrate these practices into your life. Technology offers a wealth of tools, from apps to online courses, that guide you through meditation exercises. Apps like Headspace and Calm provide a library of guided sessions catering to beginners and seasoned practitioners. These apps offer various meditation techniques, from quick breathing exercises to longer, more immersive experiences. They also include features like sleep stories, nature sounds, and daily reminders, supporting your practice and encouraging regular engagement. With these resources, you can tailor your mindfulness journey to fit your lifestyle, ensuring that peace and presence are always within reach.

7.4 BRAIN FITNESS: KEEPING YOUR MIND SHARP

Assume your brain as a garden, flourishing with vibrant thoughts and ideas. Keeping this garden thriving requires regular tending, and that's where brain fitness comes into play. Engaging your mind is crucial for maintaining sharpness and mental acuity. As we age, it's natural for cognitive function to shift, but the good news is that there are countless activities to help keep your mind agile and resilient. Cognitive exercises are a great starting point. They enhance memory and concentration, much like how daily watering and sunlight support the growth of a garden. Solving puzzles, such as crosswords or Sudoku, can be challenging and satisfying, offering a mental workout that strengthens neural connections. These activities require focus and strategy, pushing your brain to think in new ways.

In addition to puzzles, reflect on the benefits of playing strategic games. Chess, for instance, is a classic game that tests your ability to plan ahead and anticipate your opponent's moves. If chess seems daunting, card games like bridge or even digital strategy games can provide similar cognitive stimulation. These games encourage problem-solving and critical thinking, keeping your mind nimble and engaged. For a different challenge, learning a new language or musical instrument offers a double benefit: you acquire a new skill and give your brain a comprehensive workout. Language learning involves memorization and understanding complex grammar while playing an instrument requires coordination and timing. These activities stimulate different areas of the brain, promoting overall cognitive health and offering a sense of accomplishment.

Lifelong learning plays a pivotal role in brain fitness, and the options are virtually limitless. Engaging in continued education keeps your mind active, whether through enrolling in workshops, attending lectures, or taking online courses. The process of learning something new is invigorating, sparking curiosity and enthusiasm. Perhaps you've always wanted to delve into a subject like art history or astronomy—now is the perfect time. These educational pursuits provide structure and purpose, expanding your knowledge and opening doors to new interests and communities. With the rise of digital learning platforms, you can easily access courses from top universities around the world, all from the comfort of your home. This global classroom offers a wealth of opportunities to explore topics that pique your interest and keep your brain active.

Social engagement is another powerful tool for maintaining cognitive health. Interacting with others stimulates brain function and fosters a sense of connection and belonging. Participating in group discussions or clubs can be particularly beneficial. Book clubs, for example, offer a chance to dive into literature and engage in thought-provoking conversations with fellow readers. These discussions challenge your perceptions and encourage you to consider diverse perspectives. Joining a debate club or a philosophy group provides an intellectual arena where ideas are exchanged and challenged, promoting critical thinking and mental agility. The social aspect of these interactions cannot be overstated; the camaraderie and exchange of ideas invigorate the mind, creating a dynamic environment for cognitive growth.

For those looking to combine physical and mental activities, ponder joining a dance class or a tai chi group. These activities require coordination and memorization, engaging body and mind in a harmonious dance. Not only do they provide physical benefits, but they also encourage social interaction and mental focus. The rhythm of movement and the joy of learning new steps offer a holistic approach to wellness, nurturing cognitive and physical health. In this way, brain fitness becomes a multifaceted endeavor, enriching your life with knowledge, creativity, and connection. Through these diverse activities, you cultivate a garden of mental well-being, ensuring that your mind remains vibrant and resilient throughout the years.

7.5 STRESS REDUCTION TECHNIQUES FOR A PEACEFUL LIFE

Picture a tightrope stretched across two buildings, the sky a vast expanse above, and the bustling city below. Walking this line of balance can feel much like managing the stress of daily life. Chronic stress is no small adversary; it weaves itself into our physical and mental well-being, impacting everything from cardiovascular health to emotional stability. When stress takes hold, it can cause your heart to race and your blood pressure to rise, straining your cardiovascular system and increasing the risk of heart disease. The body's natural response to stress, known as the fight or flight reaction, floods your system with adrenaline. While this can be helpful in short bursts, prolonged exposure can lead to fatigue, anxiety, and even depression.

Think about incorporating practical stress reduction techniques into your daily life to step back from this precipice. One effective method is progressive muscle relaxation. This involves tensing and then slowly releasing each muscle group, starting from your toes and working your way up to your head. The act of focusing on each muscle, in turn, can distract your mind from stressors, promoting a sense of serenity and restfulness. As you release tension, your body sends signals to your brain that it's time to relax, which can help lower your heart rate and blood pressure. This simple yet powerful exercise can be done in just a few minutes, offering a respite whenever stress begins to build.

Journaling is another valuable tool for processing emotions and managing stress. Think of it as a conversation with yourself, a space where you can pour out your thoughts without judgment. Writing about your worries and frustrations allows you to externalize them, making them feel more manageable. As you write, you may discover patterns in your thoughts or solutions that were previously obscured. Journaling also provides an opportunity to reflect on positive experiences and express gratitude, shifting your focus away from stressors and fostering a more balanced perspective. Whether you prefer to jot down a few lines each day or pen longer entries when needed, the act of writing can bring clarity and relief.

Incorporating tranquility into your daily routine doesn't require grand gestures. It's about finding small pockets of time when you can retreat and recharge. Schedule regular "me-time" for activities that bring you joy and peace, whether it's a warm bath, a quiet moment with a book, prayer, or simply sitting in silence. Examine these intervals as essential as any other appointment, allowing yourself to step away from the pressures of the day. By making relaxation a priority, you create a buffer against stress, equipping yourself to handle challenges with greater ease and resilience.

Hobbies play a pivotal role in stress management, providing a creative outlet and a form of escapism. Engaging in activities that you enjoy can significantly reduce stress levels. Whether it's painting, crafting, or gardening, these pursuits demand focus and engagement, drawing your attention away from stressors and immersing you in the present moment. Creative outlets activate the right hemisphere of the brain, responsible for imagination and intuition, fostering a sense of play and exploration. This shift from analytical thinking to creative expression can alleviate stress, offering a refreshing perspective on life's challenges. As you immerse yourself in the colors of a canvas or the textures of fabric, you find a sanctuary where stress cannot easily intrude.

Creating a stress-reduction plan is a proactive step toward cultivating peace in your life. Give thought to setting aside time each day for the activities that calm and center you. Reflect on what brings you joy and balance, and make these practices a regular part of your routine. Allow yourself the freedom to experiment with different techniques, discovering what resonates with you. As you integrate these practices into your life, you'll likely find that the tightrope of stress becomes less daunting, replaced by a path that feels steady and sure.

7.6 EMBRACING A HOLISTIC APPROACH TO WELLBEING

Imagine your well-being as a beautifully intertwined tapestry, where each thread represents a different aspect of your life—physical, mental, and emotional. This interconnectedness forms the foundation of holistic health, which emphasizes the integration of body, mind, and spirit. By nurturing these elements collectively, you create a harmonious balance that supports overall wellness. A holistic approach recognizes that proper health extends beyond the absence of illness, aiming instead for a dynamic state where every part of your being thrives. It's about understanding how your emotions influence your physical state, how mental clarity can enhance your emotional resilience, and how spiritual practices can ground and center you.

Adopting a holistic lifestyle invites you to incorporate practices that honor this interconnectedness. Yoga and tai chi are excellent examples, offering gentle yet powerful ways to achieve physical and mental balance. These practices focus on breath control, flexibility, and mindful movement, fostering a deep connection between your body and mind. As you move through each pose or sequence, you cultivate awareness and inner peace, releasing tension and promoting vitality. Similarly, exploring alternative therapies like acupuncture or aromatherapy can enhance your holistic journey. Acupuncture, with its roots in traditional Chinese medicine, aims to restore energy flow and balance within the body. Aromatherapy, meanwhile, uses essential oils to uplift mood, reduce stress, and support emotional healing. By incorporating these practices into your routine, you create a holistic environment that nurtures every aspect of your well-being.

Self-awareness is a mainstay of holistic health, empowering you to understand and meet your personal needs. This awareness requires introspection and reflection, allowing you to identify areas of imbalance or distress. Techniques such as prayer or meditation can guide you in this exploration, providing clarity and insight. Journaling offers a space to articulate thoughts and emotions, uncovering patterns and triggers that may impact your well-being. Meditation invites stillness and presence, encouraging you to listen to your inner voice and align your actions with your true self. By engaging in these reflective practices, you develop a deeper connection to your needs and desires, fostering a sense of empowerment and self-compassion.

A commitment to holistic wellness is an ongoing journey, one that requires regular attention and adjustment. Just as you might schedule a health check-up, consider conducting regular check-ins with yourself to monitor and adjust your wellness practices. These moments of reflection allow you to assess what is working, what needs tweaking, and where you might introduce new elements to enhance your well-being. Perhaps you've noticed that daily meditation has brought increased peacefulness or that a particular yoga class invigorates your spirit. Celebrate these successes and remain open to exploring new avenues when needed. Remember, holistic wellness is not a destination but a continuous process that evolves with you, adapting to your changing needs and circumstances.

By embracing a holistic approach, you cultivate a rich, balanced, and fulfilling life. This perspective invites you to view health as a dynamic interplay between all facets of your being, encouraging growth and transformation. As you weave these practices into your daily life, you build a resilient foundation that supports your well-being, nurturing body and soul. Each choice you make reflects a commitment to living with intention and vitality, creating a blend of wellness that enhances every aspect of your existence.

8

EMBRACING TECHNOLOGY AND INNOVATION

R emember the first time you rode a bicycle. At first, it seemed daunting, perhaps even intimidating. But with each pedal, you grew more confident until the ride felt like second nature. In today's digital age, technology can feel just as intimidating, yet it holds the potential to enrich our lives in countless ways. Embracing technology during retirement opens doors to new experiences, connections, and conveniences. Technology is a powerful tool, whether it's keeping in touch with family, exploring hobbies, or managing daily tasks. Yet, like that first bicycle ride, it requires a bit of patience and practice to master.

8.1 BECOMING A SILVER SURFER: TECHNOLOGY BASICS FOR BEGINNERS

Let's start by demystifying the world of smartphones and tablets. Much like our old address books or photo albums, these devices have become essential companions in our daily lives. A simple swipe or tap allows you to connect with loved ones, capture precious moments, and explore new ideas. Navigating these devices begins with understanding the basic gestures: swiping to move through screens, pinching to zoom in and out, and tapping to select items. As you grow more comfortable, you'll discover a wealth of apps designed to simplify tasks and entertain. For those just beginning their journey with these devices, review exploring the settings menu, where you can adjust font sizes for easier reading or enable voice commands to assist with hands-free operation.

Moving on to computers, understanding standard software can be a game-changer. Programs like Microsoft Word or Google Docs allow you to write letters, create to-do lists, and even share documents with friends or family across the globe. These platforms often include templates that simplify tasks, from crafting a holiday newsletter to organizing a volunteer event. Learning to navigate these programs involves recognizing icons and understanding basic functions like saving, printing, and formatting text. Don't hesitate to explore the help sections or tutorials that many software programs offer, as they provide step-by-step guidance tailored to beginners.

Setting up and using an email account is another essential skill, akin to opening a virtual post office box. Email allows you to send and receive messages instantly, whether you're sharing a quick note with a friend or receiving essential updates from a community group. Begin by choosing a provider like Gmail or Yahoo, which offers user-friendly interfaces. The setup process typically involves creating a unique username and password, followed by a few security questions to protect your account. Once set up, familiarize yourself with composing emails, attaching files, and organizing your inbox using folders or labels. As you grow confident, you'll find that email becomes a vital tool for staying connected and informed.

Internet browsing is much like flipping through the pages of a vast library, each click opening new worlds of information. Start by selecting a web browser, such as Chrome, Edge, or Firefox, and practice entering web addresses or using search engines to find information. As you browse, you'll encounter hyperlinks—underlined words or phrases that, when clicked, transport you to related content. Understanding how to navigate forward and backward through pages, bookmark favorite sites, and recognize secure websites is key. Always be cautious about entering personal information and ensure that you are on trusted sites before making purchases or sharing sensitive details.

Feeling apprehensive about technology is natural, especially when faced with unfamiliar devices or software. Overcoming this anxiety begins with approaching technology as a learning opportunity rather than a challenge. Start by exploring troubleshooting strategies, such as restarting your device if it isn't working correctly or consulting online forums for solutions. Reflect on enrolling in tech workshops specifically designed for seniors, where you can learn in a supportive environment. Programs like Cyber-Seniors, which connect older adults with tech-savvy volunteers, offer free workshops and one-on-one assistance to help you gain confidence and skills.

For those eager to delve deeper, numerous resources can guide you in expanding your digital literacy. Free online tutorials and community classes, often available through local libraries or senior centers, provide structured learning opportunities. Websites like Senior Planet offer courses on a range of topics, from using social media to managing digital photos. These resources cater to various skill levels, allowing you to progress at your own pace. Whether you're mastering the basics or exploring advanced topics, the key is to remain curious and open to the possibilities that technology offers.

8.2 APPS FOR HEALTH AND WELLNESS: YOUR DIGITAL COACH

In the realm of personal wellness, technology has become a valuable ally, offering a range of apps designed to support physical, mental, and emotional health. Visualize having a personal trainer, nutritionist, and meditation guru all tucked into a device that fits in your pocket. This is the promise of health and wellness apps, which empower you to take control of your well-being with just a few taps. Fitness tracking apps like Fitbit or MyFitnessPal act as your digital fitness companions, allowing you to monitor physical activity, set exercise goals, and track progress over time. These apps can record daily steps, calories burned, and even sleep patterns, providing a comprehensive view of your physical health. With their user-friendly interfaces, they make it easy to visualize your achievements and stay motivated on your fitness journey.

When it comes to mental and emotional wellness, apps like Calm or Headspace serve as digital sanctuaries, offering guided meditation sessions that help reduce stress and promote mindfulness. These apps cater to beginners and experienced practitioners, providing a variety of courses and exercises that fit into any schedule. Whether you're seeking a moment of peace during a hectic day or establishing a regular meditation practice, these apps offer tools that cultivate a sense of inner peace and balance. Their soothing voices and tranquil music create an atmosphere conducive to restfulness, making them a delightful addition to your daily routine. By integrating these practices, you create space for reflection and rejuvenation, enhancing your overall well-being.

Choosing the right app can feel overwhelming with so many options available. Start by considering your personal health goals and the specific features you need. User-friendliness is key; look for apps with intuitive navigation that simplify your experience.

Customer reviews can also offer insights into an app's effectiveness and reliability. Pay attention to feedback from users who share similar goals or challenges as you. Additionally, explore apps that align with your lifestyle, whether you need reminders for hydration, guidance for nutrition, or tools for stress management. Prioritizing apps that offer personalized recommendations ensures that the tools you choose genuinely support your wellness journey.

Integrating these digital tools into your daily habits is an empowering step toward achieving your wellness goals. Set reminders for exercise or hydration to ensure these activities become part of your routine. Many apps offer customizable notifications that gently prompt you to move, drink water, or take a mindful break. These reminders act as nudges, keeping you on track and reinforcing positive habits. Use the tracking features to celebrate small victories, whether that's meeting a step goal or completing a meditation session. By acknowledging these achievements, you build momentum and confidence, inspiring continued progress.

To illustrate the power of these tools, contemplate creating a personalized wellness plan that incorporates various apps. Start by identifying your primary health objectives, such as improving fitness, reducing stress, or enhancing sleep quality. Then, select apps that cater to each goal, ensuring they complement one another. For instance, pair a fitness app with a nutrition tracker to gain a holistic view of your physical health. Simultaneously, integrate a meditation app to support emotional well-being. This tailored approach allows you to address multiple aspects of wellness, creating a balanced and comprehensive plan that adapts to your evolving needs.

Visual Element: App Selection Checklist

Consider using a checklist to help you choose the right apps. List your health goals and essential features you desire in an app, such as tracking capabilities, user interface, and community support. Check user reviews and ratings to gauge satisfaction. Evaluate free trials or basic versions before committing to premium options. This checklist will guide your selection and ensure you find apps that resonate with your lifestyle and aspirations.

8.3 ONLINE LEARNING PLATFORMS: EXPANDING YOUR HORIZONS

Imagine sitting comfortably at home, sipping your morning coffee, as you explore a world of knowledge available at your fingertips. This is the promise of online learning platforms like Coursera, edX, and Khan Academy. These websites offer an expansive range of courses, covering everything from ancient history to advanced computer science. Whether you're rekindling an old interest or diving into an entirely new field, these platforms provide the resources you need. Specialized platforms also cater to artistic pursuits, offering lessons in painting, music, and even creative writing, allowing you to nurture your talents and passions with expert guidance.

The beauty of online education lies in its flexibility. Unlike traditional classrooms, digital learning allows you to set your own pace. You can pause, rewind, and revisit lectures whenever you wish, making it ideal for those who learn best through repetition. This self-directed pace can relieve the pressure of strict deadlines, letting you absorb information in a manner that suits you best. Additionally, these platforms bring global universities right into your living room. Suppose you are taking a course from a prestigious institution without the need to travel. This access to diverse perspectives enriches your understanding and broadens your horizons, connecting you with a global community of learners.

When selecting courses, it's essential to choose ones that resonate with your interests and align with your skill level. Start by browsing course catalogs and reading detailed descriptions. Pay attention to prerequisites to ensure you have the foundational knowledge needed to succeed. Reviews from past students can also provide valuable insights into the course's quality and relevance. These reviews often highlight the strengths and weaknesses of the course, offering a candid look at what you can expect. By taking the time to research and select courses thoughtfully, you maximize your learning experience and ensure it is both rewarding and enjoyable.

Active engagement in online learning can significantly enhance your experience. Rather than passively consuming content, seek out opportunities to interact with fellow learners. Many platforms offer discussion forums where you can ask questions, share insights, and engage in meaningful dialogue. These forums create a sense of community, allowing you to connect with others who share your interests. Additionally, think about joining study groups, either virtually or locally, to further enrich your learning. Collaborating with others deepens your understanding and provides accountability, helping you stay committed to your educational goals.

Setting personal learning objectives is another way to make the most of your online education. Start by outlining what you hope to achieve with each course. These objectives can be specific, such as mastering a particular skill, or more general, like gaining a broader understanding of a topic. By defining clear goals, you create a roadmap for your learning journey, guiding your focus and efforts. As you progress, regularly assess your progress toward these objectives. Reflecting on your achievements and areas for improvement helps you stay motivated and ensures your learning remains purposeful and aligned with your aspirations.

Interactive Element: Course Selection Worksheet

Consider creating a course selection worksheet to help you select the right courses. List the topics you're interested in exploring and note any prerequisites you might need. Include sections for course reviews and personal objectives. Use this worksheet as a guide to evaluate potential courses, ensuring they match your interests and learning goals. This structured approach helps streamline your decision-making process, making it easier to find classes that enrich your knowledge and skills.

8.4 STAYING CONNECTED: SOCIAL MEDIA AND COMMUNICATION TOOLS

Envision sitting on your patio with a glass of lemonade, while scrolling through photos of your granddaughter's birthday party or your friend's new garden. This is the magic of social media— bringing distant loved ones closer, one post at a time. Platforms like Facebook, Twitter, and Instagram offer a virtual window into the lives of family and friends, allowing you to share life updates, photos, and videos with just a few clicks. Whether it's a snapshot of your latest project or a heartfelt message to a friend across the country, these platforms keep the lines of communication open, fostering connections regardless of distance. Social media has transformed the way we interact, creating a sense of community that defies geographical boundaries.

Beyond sharing updates, social platforms offer a wealth of opportunities to engage with diverse interests and communities. You can join groups aligned with your hobbies, such as knitting clubs, book discussions, or travel forums, where you can exchange ideas and experiences with like-minded individuals. These interactions enrich your social life and provide a sense of belonging in a broader community. Additionally, social media lets you stay informed about global events, trends, and innovations, keeping you connected to the world while nurturing personal connections. It's a dynamic space where relationships thrive, supported by the constant flow of information and interaction.

In addition to social media, communication tools like Zoom and Skype have revolutionized the way we connect face-to-face, even when miles apart. These video-calling apps transform ordinary conversations into meaningful interactions, allowing you to see the smiles and hear the laughter of loved ones in real time. Picture hosting a virtual family reunion, where relatives from different parts of the world gather on a screen, sharing stories and laughter as if sitting around the same table. These tools have become invaluable, particularly in times when physical gatherings aren't possible, ensuring that the warmth of family and friendship remains uninterrupted.

Messaging apps like WhatsApp and Signal add another layer of convenience, facilitating instant communication that feels personal and immediate. Whether it's a quick hello or an in-depth conversation, these apps keep you connected through text, voice, and even video messages. They're perfect for staying in touch with friends and family, sharing moments as they happen, or coordinating plans with ease. The simplicity and accessibility of these tools make them a staple in modern communication, bridging gaps and strengthening bonds across distances. With features like group chats and media sharing, they enrich interactions and make staying in touch effortless.

As you engage with these digital tools, it's vital to prioritize privacy and security. Adjusting your privacy settings on social media controls what you share and with whom. Take the time to explore each platform's privacy options, ensuring that only trusted individuals can view your posts and updates. Be mindful of the information you share publicly and avoid posting sensitive details like your home address or travel plans. Regularly examine your friend lists and connections, keeping your network secure and personalized. Additionally, familiarize yourself with the security features of messaging apps, such as end-to-end encryption, which protects your conversations from unauthorized access.

To further safeguard your online interactions, stay informed about the potential risks associated with digital communication. Be cautious about accepting friend requests from unknown individuals and avoid clicking on suspicious links, which could lead to phishing attempts or malware. Educate yourself on recognizing scams and fraudulent events to ensure that your digital presence remains safe and secure. By staying vigilant and informed, you can enjoy the benefits of social media and communication tools while maintaining control over your online privacy.

8.5 SMART HOMES AND TECH GADGETS: CREATING A CONVENIENT LIFESTYLE

Picture this: you're sitting in your favorite armchair and with a simple voice command, the room adjusts to the perfect temperature, your favorite playlist starts, and the lights dim to a cozy hue. This scenario isn't just a vision of the future; it's the reality of smart home technology today. Smart devices like thermostats and security cameras have revolutionized our living spaces, turning them into personalized havens that cater to our needs. These devices enhance convenience and bolster safety, offering peace of mind with features like remote monitoring and alerts. Think of a smart thermostat that learns your schedule, automatically adjusting to save energy and maintain comfort. Or a security camera that keeps an eye on your home, sending notifications directly to your smartphone whenever motion is detected.

Voice-activated assistants, such as Amazon Alexa or Google Home, add another layer of ease to daily life. These devices serve as personal assistants, capable of managing everything from setting reminders to ordering groceries. Imagine waking up in the morning and asking your assistant about the weather forecast, your schedule for the day, or even a new recipe to try for dinner. With simple voice commands, you can control various smart devices throughout your home, streamlining tasks that once required multiple steps. The beauty of these assistants lies in their ability to integrate with a wide array of smart gadgets, creating a seamless ecosystem that responds to your voice.

Installing smart home technology might seem daunting, but the process is often smoother than anticipated. Begin with the basics, like setting up a smart thermostat. These devices typically come with user-friendly apps that guide you through installation. Secure the thermostat to the wall, connect it to your Wi-Fi network, and configure it through the app. Similarly, security cameras often involve mounting the camera, connecting it to a power source, and syncing it with an app for live monitoring. Voice-activated assistants usually require plugging into a power outlet, connecting to Wi-Fi, and completing a quick setup through a smartphone app. Once integrated, these devices can be customized to fit your lifestyle, ensuring they meet your preferences and needs.

As you explore smart home technology, keep an open mind to the myriads of gadgets available. Wearable tech, like smartwatches, provides valuable insights into health, tracking steps, heart rate, and even sleep patterns. These devices serve as personal health monitors, encouraging you to stay active and informed about your well-being. Consider the convenience of receiving notifications, calls, and messages right on your wrist, allowing you to stay connected without constantly checking your phone. The integration of health apps and smartwatches creates a comprehensive wellness toolkit that supports your lifestyle.

Curiosity and willingness to experiment with new technology can transform your home into a space that anticipates your needs. Whether it's automated lighting that adjusts based on the time of day or a smart fridge that suggests recipes based on its contents, these innovations simplify daily tasks and enhance quality of life. As you become more familiar with smart technology, you'll discover endless possibilities for customization, allowing each device to serve a purpose tailored to your routine. With each addition, your home becomes a more intuitive environment, fostering comfort and efficiency.

8.6 CYBERSECURITY: PROTECTING YOUR DIGITAL PRESENCE

In our increasingly digital lives, protecting personal information online has become crucial. While a gateway to convenience and connection, the internet can also be risky if not navigated with caution. Identity theft and data breaches are not just abstract threats; they can have real, tangible impacts on your life. Visualize logging into your bank account only to find your funds mysteriously depleted or receiving bills for purchases you never made. These scenarios, unfortunately, are realities for many who fall victim to online scams. It's important to understand that cybercriminals often target those they perceive as vulnerable, hoping to exploit any gaps in security. Therefore, taking proactive measures to secure your digital presence is not only wise but necessary.

Creating strong, unique passwords for all your accounts is one of the simplest yet most effective strategies to enhance your online safety. Think of your password as the key to your digital home. Would you leave your front door unlocked? Similarly, a weak password is an open invitation to cyber intruders. Use a mix of letters, numbers, and special characters to make your passwords as complex as possible. Avoid using easily guessed information like birthdays or common words. Give thought to using a password manager to keep track of your passwords securely. These tools generate and store complex passwords, so you don't have to remember each one. In addition to strong passwords, enabling two-factor authentication adds an extra layer of security. This method requires a second form of verification, such as a text message code, before granting access to your account. It's like having a deadbolt on your digital door.

Recognizing and avoiding online scams is another critical aspect of cybersecurity. Scammers are clever, often disguising their attacks to look legitimate. Be wary of emails or messages from unknown sources that request personal information or urge immediate action. Common red flags include poor grammar, urgent language, and unfamiliar email addresses. Phishing scams often mimic trusted institutions, like your bank, to trick you into revealing sensitive information. Always verify the sender's authenticity before clicking on any links or downloading attachments. When in doubt, contact the company directly using contact information from their official website. Staying informed about these tactics can empower you to recognize and avoid potential threats.

Regular updates and security practices are your best defense against cyber threats. Much like a car needs regular maintenance, your devices and software require updates to run smoothly and securely. Software updates often include patches for security vulnerabilities that, if left unaddressed, could be exploited by hackers. Set your devices to update automatically, ensuring you always have the latest protections in place. Installing reputable antivirus software is another vital practice, as it detects and neutralizes malicious software that may try to infiltrate your system. These programs run quietly in the background, offering peace of mind as you navigate the digital world. Regularly scanning your devices can catch potential threats early, preventing them from causing harm.

Textual Element: Cybersecurity Checklist

Examine using a cybersecurity checklist to bolster your digital defenses. This tool can guide you through essential steps, such as reviewing and updating your passwords, checking for software updates, and ensuring your antivirus protection is current. It also includes reminders to enable two-factor authentication and verify the authenticity of emails before responding. This checklist serves as a practical resource to reinforce your cybersecurity routine, keeping your digital presence secure and your mind at ease.

Protecting your digital footprint gives you the confidence to explore the internet's vast opportunities without fear. As you continue to engage with technology, these practices will become second nature, allowing you to focus on the digital world's positive aspects. With cybersecurity as your foundation, you are well prepared to navigate the digital landscape safely and securely, ensuring your online interactions remain positive and productive.

PASSING THE TORCH

Now that you've explored how to redefine retirement on your own terms—finding purpose, nurturing relationships, and embracing this new chapter with confidence—it's time to pay it forward.

By sharing your honest opinion of this book on Amazon, you'll guide other women to the support and inspiration they're searching for. Your review can shine a light for someone who's just beginning their journey and help her discover how to create a fulfilling retirement that's uniquely hers.

Thank you for being part of this empowering journey. Retirement is redefined when we share what we've learned—and you're helping me inspire women everywhere to approach this chapter with excitement and possibility.

Scan the QR code to leave your review on Amazon.

With appreciation,

Victoria Spring

CONCLUSION

As we close the pages of this book, I invite you to pause and reflect on our journey together. Throughout these chapters, we've explored the myriad facets of retirement, uncovering the secrets to a joyful and engaged lifestyle. We've delved into the importance of redefining your identity, achieving financial peace, nurturing social connections, and embracing the possibilities that this new chapter brings. Each insight has been a steppingstone, guiding you towards a retirement that is as unique and vibrant as you are.

The path to a fulfilling retirement is paved with self-discovery and growth. As you embark on this adventure, remember that you hold the power to shape your experience. Accept the opportunity to explore new passions, whether it's diving into a fascinating subject through online learning or unleashing your creativity through a long-forgotten hobby. These pursuits enrich your mind and foster a sense of purpose and vitality.

Financial security is the basis of a carefree retirement. By implementing the strategies discussed, such as smart budgeting and savvy investment choices, you can build a solid foundation for

enjoying your golden years with peace of mind. Remember, wealth isn't just about numbers in a bank account; it's about the freedom to live life on your terms without the burden of financial stress.

The relationships you nurture during retirement create a network of love and support. Strengthen bonds with family and form new friendships through shared interests. In life's challenges, these connections become a sanctuary of strength, laughter, and comfort. Embrace the sense of belonging that comes from community, knowing you are never alone on this journey.

As you craft your daily routines, prioritize activities that bring you joy and fulfillment. Infuse your days with purpose, whether it's through volunteering, pursuing a long-held passion, or simply savoring the beauty of a quiet moment. Remember, retirement is not about filling time; it's about living each day to its fullest, on your own terms.

Throughout this book, we've explored a myriad of ways technology can enhance your retirement experience. From staying connected with loved ones across the miles to unlocking new worlds of knowledge, these digital tools are your allies. Support the opportunities they provide, while always prioritizing your well-being and security in the online space.

As you navigate the challenges and triumphs of retirement, remember that you are the author of your own story. Each day presents a new page, waiting to be filled with the adventures, laughter, and love that you choose. Espouse the power of self-reflection, taking moments to assess your journey and adjust your course as needed. This is your time to dream big, to chase the passions that set your soul on fire, and to create a retirement that exceeds your wildest expectations.

I encourage you to take the insights and strategies from this book and weave them into the fabric of your life. Start small, implementing one change at a time, and watch as your retirement blossoms into a masterpiece of your own making. Seek out the company of other women who share your aspirations, joining online communities or local groups where you can exchange ideas, offer support, and celebrate each other's successes.

So, my dear reader, go forth with confidence and joy. The world is waiting for the unique gifts that only you can bring. Embrace this new chapter with a heart full of hope and a spirit ready for adventure. Your retirement is a story waiting to be written, and I can't wait to see the masterpiece you create.

Nurture the relationships that matter most, whether it's strengthening bonds with family or building new friendships through shared interests. In the face of life's challenges, these connections serve as a source of strength, laughter, and comfort. Champion the power of community, knowing that you are never alone on this journey.

Above all, remember that you are not alone in this journey. As you turn the final page of this book, know that I am here, cheering you on every step of the way. Your retirement is a canvas, waiting to be painted with the vibrant hues of your dreams and desires. Embrace this opportunity with open arms, knowing that the best is yet to come.

REFERENCES

Regions. (n.d.). *Rethinking retirement: 3 women share their stories*. Retrieved from https://www.regions.com/insights/personal/retirement/establishing-a-plan/ rethinking-retirement-3-women-share-their-stories

Conservatory Senior Living. (n.d.). *Personal development tips for seniors*. Retrieved from https://www.conservatoryseniorliving.com/senior-living-blog/personaldevelopment-tips-for-seniors/

Yale School of Public Health. (n.d.). *Early retirement impacts mental health of bluecollar women more than white-collar peers*. Retrieved from https://ysph.yale.edu/ news-article/retirement-impacts-mental-health-of-blue-collar-women-morethan-white-collar-peers/

Women's Institute for a Secure Retirement. (n.d.). *National Resource Center on Women and Retirement*. Retrieved from https://wiserwomen.org/nationalresource-center-on-women-and-retirement-2/

SeniorLiving.org. (n.d.). *The best budgeting apps for seniors*. Retrieved from https://www.seniorliving.org/finance/budgeting-apps/

National Council on Aging. (n.d.). *How can I boost my Social Security benefit?*. Retrieved from https://www.ncoa.org/article/get-more-money-from-socialsecurity-7-tips-to-max-out-your-benefits/

NerdWallet. (n.d.). *Best brokers for beginner investors: Top picks for 2025*. Retrieved from https://www.nerdwallet.com/best/investing/online-brokers-for-beginners

AARP. (n.d.). *15 part-time jobs for retirees (no degree required!)*. Retrieved from https://www.aarp.org/work/job-search/retiree-part-time-jobs/

Senior Helpers. (2023, April 10). *The benefits of joining a senior center or club*. Retrieved from https://www.seniorhelpers.com/or/corvallis/resources/blogs/ 2023-04-10/

Sonida Senior Living. (n.d.). *The best social media sites for seniors: A guide to staying connected and engaged*. Retrieved from https://www.sonidaseniorliving.com/thebest-social-media-sites-for-seniors-a-guide-to-staying-connected-andengaged/

Ocean of Solitude. (n.d.). *How technology is redefining long-distance friendships*. Retrieved from https://oceanofsolitude.com/how-technology-is-redefininglong-distance-friendships/

AmeriCorps. (n.d.). *AmeriCorps Seniors*. Retrieved from https://americorps.gov/ serve/americorps-seniors

Stellar Living. (n.d.). *How to create a masterful morning routine for seniors*. Retrieved from https://stellarliving.com/create-a-masterful-morning-routine/

Kiplinger. (n.d.). *9 tips for better time management in retirement*. Retrieved from https://www.kiplinger.com/retirement/601545/9-tips-for-better-time-manage ment-in-retirement

Senior Lifestyle. (n.d.). *Why lifelong learning is important for seniors*. Retrieved from https://www.seniorlifestyle.com/resources/blog/lifelong-learning-for-seniors/

Upscoop. (n.d.). *Evening reflection: The key to personal growth and success*. Retrieved from https://www.upscoop.com/evening-reflection-the-key-to-personalgrowth-and-success

Road Scholar. (n.d.). *Best retirement hobbies: Ideas for seniors over 60*. Retrieved from https://www.roadscholar.org/blog/12-best-retirement-hobbies/

Harvard Business Review. (2017, February). *Lifelong learning is good for your health, your wallet, and your social life*. Retrieved from https://hbr.org/2017/02/lifelonglearning-is-good-for-your-health-your-wallet-and-your-social-life

Independent Financial Services. (n.d.). *Encore careers: A new chapter for women in retirement*. Retrieved from https://www.ifstampabay.com/encore-careers-anew-chapter-for-women-in-retirement/

VolunteerMatch. (n.d.). *VolunteerMatch - Where volunteering begins*. Retrieved from https://www.volunteermatch.org/

Verywell Mind. (n.d.). *How to set boundaries with your adult children*. Retrieved from https://www.verywellmind.com/setting-boundaries-with-adult-children8686106

Marriage.com. (n.d.). *8 considerate ways to strengthen your marriage in retirement*. Retrieved from https://www.marriage.com/advice/marriage-fitness/ strengthen-your-marriage-in-retirement/

Greater Good Science Center. (n.d.). *How to navigate the joys and challenges of grandparenting*. Retrieved from https://greatergood.berkeley.edu/article/item/how_to_navigate_the_joys_and_challenges_of_grandparenting

Mental Health America. (n.d.). *Caregiving and the sandwich generation*. Retrieved from https://mhanational.org/caregiving-and-sandwich-generation

Senior Lifestyle. (n.d.). *7 best exercises for seniors (and a few to avoid!)*. Retrieved from https://www.seniorlifestyle.com/resources/blog/7-best-exercises-for-seniorsand-a-few-to-avoid/

MedlinePlus. (n.d.). *Nutrition for older adults*. Retrieved from https://medlineplus. gov/nutritionforolderadults.html

Wirecutter. (2025). *The 4 best meditation apps of 2025*. Retrieved from https://www. nytimes.com/wirecutter/reviews/best-meditation-apps/

National Institute on Aging. (n.d.). *Cognitive health and older adults*. Retrieved from https://www.nia.nih.gov/health/brain-health/cognitive-health-and-olderadults

Cyber-Seniors. (n.d.). *Cyber-Seniors*. Retrieved from https://cyberseniors.org/ Byvi. (2023, October 5). *Top health apps for women to master a wellness journey*. Retrieved from https://byvi.co/2023/10/05/health-apps-for-women/

Senior Planet from AARP. (n.d.). *Online classes for seniors*. Retrieved from https://seniorplanet.org/classes/

Cybersecurity and Infrastructure Security Agency. (n.d.). *Cybersecurity and older Americans*. Retrieved from https://www.cisa.gov/sites/default/files/publications/Cybersecurity%2520and%2520Older%2520Americans.pdf

RETIREMENT BEYOND FINANCES

FULFILL YOUR TIME WITH PURPOSE, ACHIEVE A
HEALTHIER AND ACTIVE LIFESTYLE, AND
CREATE SOCIAL CONNECTIONS TO EMBRACE
A NEW WAY OF LIFE

VICTORIA SPRING

INTRODUCTION

Greetings, and welcome to *Retirement Beyond Finances*, where your retirement may become a canvas for a life full of happiness and vitality! This book goes beyond the typical financial advice and serves as your passport on a journey rich in experience. Whether you are looking for a revitalized sense of purpose, activities that have significance, or the ability to be resilient in the face of adversity, we have what you need. Prepare yourself to flourish, open the door to your interests, and manage retirement with self-assurance. This book is not only a handbook but a companion on the thrilling journey of sculpting a retirement that is as abundant in meaning as it is in pleasure. Let's reinvent retirement together!

AUDIENCE

Imagine this: You are a dynamic person with a zest for life who is about to embark on an exciting new trip known as retirement. If you are reading this, you are likely either planning the early stages or already enjoying this new chapter of life. Most of our readers— a vibrant mix of men and women— are slipping into their 50s, 60s, and 70s with elegance, a generation that radiates intelligence, wisdom, and energy.

Let's discuss retirement now. Your financial ship is floating nicely, whether you are already retired and enjoying newfound independence or standing on the brink, looking into the future. The key is stability, and we are aware that you are designing a lifestyle that realizes your goals and objectives rather than just looking to retire. You are here to make the most of a new adventure, not dwell on the ordinary.

Let's be honest: retirement is not only about 401(k)s and pension plans but also about pursuing your hobbies with abandon and finding joy and contentment. Every choice you make along the way colors life's canvas. We understand, too; you are used to the uncertainty surrounding retirement and the state of the economy. With the expertise to maneuver the currents and take full advantage of the tide, you want to surf those waves confidently.

The fundamental reason you are here, however, is because you are uncertain and possibly a little lost contemplating a life without work. You are not willing to accept anything less than a wonderful retirement. You want each moment to have significance and the days filled with endless possibilities. You wish to reinterpret this stage, dispel myths, and reject the cliched retirement counsel that has been.

Essentially, you are exhausted—weary of the canned advice that does not apply to your situation. You are prepared for direction from someone aware of your aspirations, anxieties, and range of feelings that come with retirement. So, here's to you—the person looking for a meaningful retirement, who rejects stereotypes, and the person who values your newfound freedom. Greetings from a book written specifically for you—a guide to retirement as unique as the adventure itself!

WHY YOU MUST READ THIS BOOK

Have you ever felt that your profession defines who you are, and the prospect of retiring makes you shudder? You are not alone! Even though our readers are successful in their careers, they face new challenges with retirement. Finding a new pace and rhythm for their life is more important than just leaving their job.

Let's accomplish our objective, achieve a healthy, active lifestyle, create new social connections, and embrace the changing nature of retirement. Come along as we transform challenges into opportunities!

BENEFITS FROM THIS BOOK

This book offers a wide range of benefits that extend beyond the financial aspects of retirement. It takes a holistic approach, focusing on nurturing all aspects of life, including health, relationships, and personal growth. Here are some key benefits that readers can expect:

- **Holistic Approach:** Emphasizes retirement and is not just about financial planning. It encourages retirees to consider their overall well-being and find balance in all areas of life. ● **Creating a Vision:** Guiding retirees to envision their ideal retirement life helps them create a clear picture of what they want their retirement to look and feel like. ● **Health and Wellness:** Recognizes the importance of physical and mental well-being during retirement. It offers guidance on exercise, healthy eating, and stress reduction techniques to ensure a rewarding and active lifestyle. ● **Meaningful Relationships:** Provides strategies for fostering and maintaining meaningful relationships with family, friends, and the community. It highlights the importance of social connections in retirement. ● **Exploration and Adventure:** Encourages retirees to embrace new experiences, hobbies, and adventures. It inspires a sense of curiosity and exploration during this phase of life.

- **Purpose and Contribution:** Helps readers accomplish their objective through volunteering, mentorship, or pursuing passion projects. It empowers retirees to contribute to causes they are passionate about. ● **Transitioning Successfully:** Offers practical tips and advice on navigating the emotional and psychological transition into retirement. Assists individuals in adjusting to a new phase of life.

- **Creating a Legacy:** Guides retirees to reflect on their life's legacy with guidance on making a lasting impact through their values, wisdom, and contributions to future generations.

These benefits aim to provide retirees with a comprehensive guide to ensure financial stability and live an enthusiastic, fulfilling, and vibrant life during their retirement years.

IGNITE YOUR RETIREMENT JOURNEY WITH OUR BOOK!

Prepare to discover the keys to embracing a new way of life.

- Learn unconventional tactics—this book is a road map to discovering hidden interests, getting to know yourself better, and reaching long-held objectives.
- Hold on, though—we are not going to stop there. This is not an average retirement handbook. Our goal is for you to discover! Discover abilities, explore passions, and personalize your goals for the future.

- As you turn the last page, prepare for a renewed spark. Our book is a catalyst for change, not merely something to read. Imagine having routines that keep your inner fire burning, enriching activities effortlessly incorporated into a new lifestyle that is not just lived but looked forward to!

Welcome retirement with unparalleled joy. Come along on this journey of self-discovery, pursuing passions, and creating a retirement that is all YOURS!

MEET VICTORIA SPRING - YOUR RETIREMENT GUIDE

Victoria is passionate about helping people make informed decisions about their retirement options. Her enthusiasm is driven by her conviction that every person deserves a life filled with meaning and a worry-free retirement. She hopes to empower people with the right tools and understanding to navigate their journey effectively.

FIRST STEP INTO YOUR FUTURE

The first chapter kicks off an exciting journey to reimagine what retirement means. As you turn the page, be prepared to investigate various methods, activities, and insights that might be of assistance in welcoming the future with newfound enthusiasm. Join us in establishing a thriving retirement community brimming with happiness and a sense of achievement. At this moment, your new chapter starts!

THE ABCS OF RETIREMENT

"Retire from work, but not from life."

— M.K. SONI

RETIREMENT MYTHS: NURTURING MENTAL WELL-BEING BEYOND FINANCES

The concept of retirement, often depicted as a peaceful sanctuary, can be complicated by preconceived notions that go beyond financial matters and significantly impact one's emotional well-being. It is time to dispel these outdated ideas by focusing on financial concerns and the crucial components of mental health.

Myth 1: Retirement means the end of productivity: Research has shown that keeping mentally active during retirement is vital for a satisfying post-work life (Smith & Agronin, 2019). This contradicts the common belief that retirement signifies the end of one's productive contributions. Engaging in activities like volunteering or pursuing hobbies can significantly contribute to one's mental well-being and instill a sense of accomplishment.

Myth 2: Financial planning is the sole determinant of retirement happiness: While financial planning is undoubtedly essential, concentrating entirely on monetary matters can be a source of stress, as highlighted by Financial Mentor (n.d.). A successful retirement requires more than just financial considerations. Prioritizing emotional well-being through nurturing social relationships and activities that bring joy is critical.

Myth 3: Retirement is a one-size-fits-all experience: Every individual's retirement experience is unique. As Great Eastern Life (n.d.) emphasizes, mental well-being in retirement should be personalized based on individual interests and preferences. Whether a peaceful retirement community or a bustling urban lifestyle, tailoring the experience to align with personal goals and objectives ensures a positive mindset.

Myth 4: Retirement must occur at a predetermined age: The notion that retirement should happen at a fixed age is no longer relevant. According to Aspen Wealth Management (n.d.), deciding when to retire should be a personal choice based on individual circumstances to promote a sense of purpose and achievement.

Myth 5: Constant busyness equates to happiness in retirement: While maintaining an active lifestyle is essential, striking a balance between activities and moments of relaxation is equally crucial (Western & Southern, n.d.). Constant busyness without any moments of rest can lead to stress and burnout, negatively impacting mental well-being.

In conclusion, to break free from retirement misconceptions, it is necessary to take a holistic approach that goes beyond financial worries. By embracing the diverse experiences that retirement offers, maintaining a flexible mindset, and prioritizing mental well-being, it is possible to have a retirement that provides financial security and a joyful chapter in life.

THE UNVEILING OF RETIREMENT - A JOURNEY THROUGH ITS STAGES

The process of retirement, often seen as a single event, actually unfolds in a series of distinct stages, each characterized by its own set of events and emotions. Let's delve deeper into these stages, as described by various experts and resources:

Pre-retirement—Anticipation and planning: As Investopedia (n.d.) outlined, the period leading up to retirement is filled with anticipation and meticulous planning. Individuals may experience a range of emotions, from excitement to fear, as they anticipate this significant life transition. During this phase, making lifestyle adjustments, setting personal goals, and considering financial implications are crucial.

The big day - A momentous transition: The day of retirement marks the end of one chapter and the beginning of a new one, a truly meaningful transition. According to the Second Wind Movement (n.d.), this day holds great significance for many as it symbolizes freedom and accomplishment. However, it may also evoke feelings of uncertainty as individuals navigate the uncharted territory of post-retirement life.

Honeymoon phase - The blissful beginning: The honeymoon phase is characterized by a sense of happiness and freedom, often lasting for months or even years, as noted by Wild Pine Residence (n.d.). During this period, retirees relish their newfound leisure time, experiment with new activities, and enjoy the absence of work-related stress. It is a leisure and pleasure time akin to a second youth.

Disenchantment - Facing reality: Some retirees may eventually experience a period of disillusionment as the honeymoon phase ends (Investopedia, n.d.).

The initial excitement of retirement may give way to feelings of being adrift or bored. This stage emphasizes the importance of a well-considered retirement plan that includes meaningful activities to maintain a sense of achievement.

Reorientation—Finding a new purpose: According to the Second Wind Movement, reorientation is a critical stage during which retirees have the opportunity to reassess their priorities, redefine their goals, and seek a renewed sense of motivation. It involves accepting retirement as a new reality and exploring other paths contributing to personal contentment and overall wellbeing.

Routine—Establishing a new normal: The routine stage entails settling into a more structured lifestyle, as Wild Pine Residence describes. This may involve developing daily routines, consistently engaging in activities, and nurturing social relationships. Striking a balance between leisure and structure becomes increasingly essential for a satisfying retirement.

Retirement is a multi-faceted journey that progresses through phases of anticipation, freedom, joy, challenges, rejuvenation, and, ultimately, establishing a new normal. Recognizing and understanding these stages can help individuals navigate the transitions more effectively, ensuring a diverse and fulfilling retirement experience.

CROSSING THE SEAS OF RETIREMENT: IDENTIFYING AND MITIGATING KEY RISKS

Retirement is often seen as a time of relaxation and leisure but comes with its fair share of financial challenges. It is essential to be aware of risks and make the necessary preparations to ensure a safe and stress-free retirement. Let's explore some common retirement hazards and strategies for managing them:

Riding the financial waves: Changes in the market can pose a significant risk to retirement funds. To mitigate risk, diversify your financial portfolio. This means having a mix of assets like stocks, bonds, and other investments to distribute the risk and enhance stability.

Outliving your savings: With increasing life expectancy, there is a possibility of outliving retirement funds. Thorough preparation is vital to combat this. Examine financial products like annuities that provide a steady source of income throughout your life.

Eroding purchasing power: Inflation can decrease the buying power of retirement income over time. To combat this, invest in assets historically proven to outpace inflation, such as stocks. Regularly evaluate and adjust your retirement plan to keep up with the rising cost of living.

Unforeseen medical expenses: Rising healthcare costs can be a significant concern for retirees. Comprehensive health insurance and a health savings account (HSA) can help prepare for potential medical expenses.

Timing matters: The order in which investment returns occur can impact retirement savings. Early retirement with low returns can have long-lasting effects. To manage this risk, have a combination of growth-oriented and conservative assets, and think about working with a financial adviser to navigate market unpredictability.

Striking the right balance: Taking too much money from retirement savings can deplete them early. Determine a manageable and sustainable withdrawal rate that allows funds to last throughout retirement. When calculating this rate, contemplate various factors like lifestyle, projected costs, and market conditions.

Effectively preparing for retirement requires awareness of the risks involved and the ability to navigate them. Diversifying assets, preparing for longevity, considering inflation, addressing healthcare costs, controlling the sequence of returns, and adopting an adequate withdrawal strategy can help individuals approach retirement with confidence and financial stability.

FACING THE REALITY: THE HARD TRUTHS ABOUT RETIREMENT

Although retirement is often portrayed as a peaceful chapter in one's life, it can come with its fair share of difficulties, especially when considering leaving employment earlier than expected. Let's have a look at some of the hidden features that people need to understand and accept to go forward:

Social isolation - A potential loneliness factor: According to Money Smart Guides (n.d.), after retirement, you may experience feelings of social isolation, particularly if your social life is predominantly centered on your place of employment. When overcoming feelings of isolation, having a healthy social network outside of the workplace is necessary. Participate in hobbies, volunteer work, or join groups designed to help build new relationships.

Loss of identity - Beyond the job title: For many people, the workplace is a crucial factor in determining who they are. According to HelpGuide (n.d.), early retirement might result in a loss of identity and enthusiasm in one's life. The best way to deal with this situation is to think about trying new hobbies, becoming involved in volunteer work, or following interests that provide a fresh feeling of significance and success.

Financial strain—The reality of budgeting: Early retirement might burden one's finances since the nest egg needs to be sustained longer. Building a sustainable budget is essential for a realistic financial preparedness assessment. Seeking the help of professionals in the financial industry may give direction on prudently managing resources (Go Banking Rates, n.d.).

Healthcare costs—A growing concern: According to the National Institutes of Health Federal Credit Union (n.d.), the cost of medical care may be quite a hardship in retirement if one retires before becoming eligible for Medicare programs. The costs of healthcare should be planned, insurance choices should be investigated, and health savings accounts (HSAs) should be reviewed by early retirees to meet any prospective medical bills.

Adjustment period—The struggle to adapt: According to Yahoo Finance (n.d.), reconciling the newly acquired independence that comes with retirement might be challenging. As a result of the adjustment, you can feel restless or even bored. Plans should be made in advance for how to spend your time, establishing reasonable expectations and progressively adding things that provide a sense of attainment.

Unpredictable future—Economic and personal changes: According to The Motley Fool (n.d.), the future is unclear, and unanticipated economic or personal development may affect retirement planning. Early retirees should reevaluate their financial condition regularly, be knowledgeable about changes in the economy, and maintain the ability to adjust to unforeseen life events.

Longevity risk—Balancing enjoyment and sustainability: There is a delicate balance between enjoying the current moment and maintaining financial sustainability for a possibly lengthy retirement (The Motley Fool, n.d.). Although early retirement provides more leisure time, it is essential to remember that this balance is necessary. Engaging in careful financial planning, including reevaluating withdrawal plans, is essential.

Confronting the problematic facts about retirement, especially when deciding to retire early, is vital for a well-rounded and meaningful post-career life. If individuals acknowledge and prepare for the possibility of social, identity, financial, and lifestyle modifications, they can approach retirement with realistic expectations and develop a basis for a rewarding and secure future.

THE EMOTIONAL LANDSCAPE OF RETIREMENT – A MINDFUL TRANSITION

In addition to the exhilaration often associated with retirement, it may bring up unforeseen emotional issues. People may overlook the potential stress of such a huge life transition because they are excited about the newfound independence. Taking into consideration each step of the transition to retirement and providing general advice for a more seamless emotional trip, let's investigate how to move to retirement psychologically:

Anticipation - Recognizing the emotional impact: When they think of retirement, most individuals are excited because they see days filled with activities that satisfy them and provide them with the opportunity to rest. According to Global View Investment Advisors (2012), it is of the highest significance to recognize the emotional impact that this transition would have on the individual. Be aware of the spectrum of emotions that may arise when you say goodbye to the well-established work routine. These emotions may include feelings of excitement, dread, and even a sense of loss. Acknowledging these sentiments is necessary.

Preparation - Setting realistic expectations: Setting expectations that align with reality is integral to being ready for retirement (New Retirement, n.d.). It is significant to realize that the transition is not just about making financial preparations but also about psychologically preparing for a new chapter of life. Take some time to think about objectives, interests, and ambitions, and ensure they align with your retirement plan.

The early days - Embracing the change: According to Seasons Retirement Communities (n.d.), it is common for individuals to experience a range of feelings during the first few days of retirement. These days may offer a rush of freedom and delight. Take advantage of the change and give yourself time to acclimate to a new daily routine. Celebrate the newly acquired flexibility and put it to use by engaging in pursuits that provide a sense of accomplishment.

Emotional challenges - Addressing feelings of loss: Some people may struggle with feelings of loss as retirement approaches, mainly if their identity is strongly related to their work (Here to Help, n.d.). This is especially true for those who have been successful in their careers. Accepting these feelings and seeking assistance from friends, family, or even professional counselors who can offer guidance during this transitional time is crucial. These individuals can help navigate this moment of change.

Building new routines - Establishing structure: To maintain a feeling of determination and organization, it is essential to develop new routines (Life Matters Financial Planning, n.d.). Maintaining social connections and warding off feelings of isolation may be accomplished by participating in activities that you are enthusiastic about, volunteering, or even working part-time.

General tips for a smooth transition:

- **Stay socially connected:** Maintain social connections by cultivating contacts outside the job. Participate in social activities, get involved in neighborhood group activities, join volunteer groups, or volunteer to construct a solid support network.
- **Plan meaningful activities:** Find hobbies or activities that delight and give you a sense of accomplishment, and plan meaningful activities around them. A sense of purpose is one of the most critical factors in healthy mental wellbeing.
- **Stay physically active:** Regular physical exercise is helpful for one's health and may also improve one's mood and decrease stress. A daily regimen should include some kind of physical activity.

- **Financial wellness:** Maintaining financial well-being requires continually monitoring and modifying your financial strategy. Being aware of your current financial condition will help with feelings of anxiousness or doubt about the future.

- **Consider professional guidance:** During this time of transition, it may be beneficial to seek the guidance of financial planners, counselors, or retirement coaches to get valuable insights and support.

A Mindful Retirement Transition

Even though retirement is eagerly anticipated, it is necessary to take a conscious approach to the mental and emotional components of the transition. If individuals acknowledge and deftly handle the many emotions throughout each step of the process, they can create a positive mentality and embrace retirement with passion, intention, and a well-balanced mental state.

WISDOM FROM THOSE WHO'VE WALKED THE PATH - WHAT I WISH I KNEW BEFORE RETIRING

Even though retirement is celebrated, it has its own unique set of difficulties and surprises. Learning from others who have experienced it firsthand makes it possible to get significant ideas. The following are some of the things that people wish they had known before they retired and some of the advice they have to offer:

- **Unexpected expenses - Be financially prepared:** It is common for retirees to express the desire for better financial preparations for unforeseen expenditures (New Retirement, n.d.). You can assist in softening the effect of unanticipated financial issues by maintaining a healthy emergency fund and frequently reevaluating your budget. This can help with anything from the price of healthcare to the costs of property maintenance.

- **The importance of social connections - Cultivate relationships:** According to Forbes (2020), successful retirees underline the value of taking the time to cultivate social ties. Retirement may bring forth unanticipated challenges, such as feelings of loneliness and isolation. To construct a supporting network that adds to overall general well-being, actively participate in social events, join groups, or volunteer wherever possible.

- **The need for routine - Establish structure:** According to Honest Money (n.d.), retirees often mention establishing a routine as another piece of advice. In the beginning, the independence that comes with retirement may seem freeing; nevertheless, without structure, it may lead to a feeling of no direction. Make a daily or weekly calendar containing enjoyable things to balance leisure and structure.

- **Health and wellness - Prioritize self-care:** Many retirees regret not prioritizing their health before retirement (Quora, n.d.). Physical and mental health are vital for a satisfying retirement. Participate in regular physical activity, adhere to a well-balanced diet, and be proactive with healthcare requirements.

- **Diverse interests - Explore new passions:** An emotion shared by those reflecting on their journey through retirement is the desire to discover new interests (Living Confidently, n.d.). The option to pursue hobbies or activities you have always wanted to do becomes an option during retirement age. Seize the opportunity to learn about new passions and take pleasure in the enrichment these new pursuits bring into your life. The website 48days.com helps people transition into the work they love in 48 days.

- **Financial planning - Seek professional guidance:** Based on Inspired by Insiders (n.d.) findings, a significant number of retirees underline the significance of receiving expert financial counsel. A financial adviser can assist in navigating the complexity of retirement planning, ensure that your financial portfolio aligns with objectives, and create peace of mind as you move into this new period of life.

To summarize, the experience and knowledge of other retirees may provide valuable lessons to those who are getting close to reaching this milestone. By implementing these ideas into your retirement plan, you may contribute to a more rewarding and well-balanced existence when your job has ended. These insights range from being financially prepared to elevating the importance of social ties and self-care.

As we turn the page to Chapter Two, we set out on a path of rebirth and change. Here, find 'Stepping into the Next Chapter: Embracing a New Beginning.' As we begin this exciting new chapter in our lives, let's embrace the opportunities that lie ahead.

STEPPING INTO THE NEXT CHAPTER: EMBRACING A NEW BEGINNING

"Don't simply retire from something; have something to retire to."

— HARRY EMERSON FOSDICK

LIFE PRIORITIES IN RETIREMENT: CRAFTING MEANINGFUL PLANS

Retirement is a chance to realign life priorities for a meaningful and ambitious post-career period, not merely a financial milestone. Let us examine the key concerns in life that readers should think about while making retirement plans:

Stable income is essential for financial security: The primary goal of retirement planning should be to ensure financial stability (Kolluri & Hutchins, 2017). This entails controlling spending, generating a steady source of income, and preparing for unanticipated financial difficulties.

Physical and mental well-being - Achieving health and wellness: Making health and well-being a top priority is essential for a happy retirement. This entails leading a healthy lifestyle, getting the treatment you need, and developing mental wellness via hobbies or meditation, among other things.

Social connections - Relationships: Retirement provides a chance to improve relationships with others. To create a feeling of community and belonging, prioritize spending time with loved ones, making new acquaintances, and engaging in events.

Personal development - Exploration and lifelong learning: Retirement is the perfect time for introspection and personal development. Follow your passion for ongoing education, take up new interests, and partake in pursuits that make you feel good about yourself.

Enjoyment and leisure - Quality of life: To improve overall quality of life, prioritize leisure and pleasure. Travel, indulge in hobbies, and enjoy joyful and relaxing activities to ensure a balanced and pleasurable retirement.

Rethinking Retirement Goals and Aspirations by Setting Savings Goals

Retirement is a process that requires careful consideration at every stage of life. This guide is designed to help individuals of different age groups rethink and set retirement goals. Reviewing these goals will allow the identification of any steps that still need to be completed or any deficiencies in your timeline.

In Your 20s and 30s: Building a Strong Foundation

Create an Emergency Fund: Building an emergency fund is essential during early adulthood. Aim to save three to six months' living expenses in a cash account. The fund acts as a safety net in case of unexpected events and sets the stage for a secure future.

Contribute to Retirement Accounts: Saving for retirement early in your career creates the advantage of compound interest. Make consistent contributions to retirement accounts like 401(k)s and IRAs. This proactive approach will lay the foundation for long-term growth and wealth accumulation.

Develop Credit: Building a solid credit history is often overlooked but crucial in your 20s and 30s. It is not just about a credit score; having a robust credit history is a financial asset. Establish responsible credit habits to secure favorable interest rates and insurance costs, setting yourself up for future financial endeavors.

In Your 40s: Fine-Tuning Objectives and Maximizing Contributions

Reassess Retirement Objectives: Your 40s are a time to reflect on and adjust retirement goals. Take into account changing priorities, preferences, and potential medical needs. Fine-tune financial goals to align with evolving personal and family situations (Indeed Editorial Team, 2023).

Maximize Contributions: Your 40s also provide an opportunity to maximize contributions through catch-up options available for those over 50. Recognize the need to accelerate retirement savings and contemplate boosting contributions to retirement accounts. This strategic move will enhance the resilience of your financial portfolio as retirement draws closer (Indeed Editorial Team, 2023).

In Your 50s: Adjusting for the Final Stretch

Tune-up Your Retirement Budget: As you approach retirement, your budget must be thoughtfully modified. Ensure that financial plans accommodate future spending patterns and desired lifestyle choices. This phase is crucial in turning a post-career vision into a concrete financial plan that aligns resources with aspirations.

Examine Healthcare Options: Healthcare considerations take center stage in your 50s. Evaluate different healthcare options and think about long-term care insurance. This forward-thinking approach acknowledges potential medical needs during retirement and integrates them into your comprehensive financial strategy.

Getting Close to Retirement: Final Preparations

Assess Debt Situation: Entering retirement without high-interest debt is a wise financial move. In the years leading up to retirement, take focused steps to strategically reduce or eliminate high interest debt. This debt management strategy will provide greater financial freedom in the post-career phase.

Complete Retirement Budget: Before retiring, review and adjust your retirement budget. Make sure it aligns with desired activities and realistic expectations. This will set the stage for a seamless transition into your post-career life.

Questions to Ask Yourself When Creating Goals

Which Retirement Lifestyle Do I Imagine? Your retirement lifestyle sets the tone for financial goals. Calculate the corresponding expenses to ensure your financial roadmap aligns with post-career aspirations.

What Medical Needs Do I Have? Anticipating and planning for future medical costs is crucial. Review insurance coverage to factor potential healthcare expenses into your retirement plan.

What Is My Retirement Schedule? Establishing a goal retirement age provides a strategic anchor for financial planning. Align your savings plan with your envisioned timeline to approach retirement objectives in a synchronized manner.

Which Will Be My Sources of Income? Diversifying sources of income is critical for financial strategy. Identify and understand possible sources such as Social Security, pensions, and investment returns. This forms the foundation of your comprehensive financial plan.

What Trajectories Would I Like to Take? In addition to personal aspirations, consider legacy and estate planning. Establishing a smooth transition of wealth to heirs impacts future generations and completes retirement planning.

This comprehensive guide provides deep insights and practical steps for retirement planning. By aligning retirement goals with life priorities and taking a proactive approach to savings at each stage of life, you can navigate the complexities of financial planning and enjoy a well-rounded post-career life.

Typical Retirement Goals: A Guide to a Happy Future

Retirement is a transformative stage; well-defined objectives are critical to a fulfilling and meaningful experience. This guide delves into typical retirement goals and the significance of setting goals in retirement, providing a roadmap for crafting a balanced and enthusiastic post-career life.

Setting Refined Retirement Goals for Maximum Fulfillment

Financial Security: Achieving stability and maintaining a good standard of living form the bedrock of retirement goals. This includes ensuring a steady source of income to cover living expenditures and guaranteeing a stress-free and financially secure postcareer life.

Health and Wellness: Mental and physical health must be prioritized for a happy retirement. Investing in medical resources ensures a high standard of living, contributing to overall happiness and well-being during the post-career phase.

Travel and Adventure: Embracing new experiences through travel and leisure pursuits adds vibrancy to retirement. Accepting spontaneity and cultivating a spirit of adventure contribute to a sense of contentment and satisfaction during this transformative period.

These typical retirement objectives provide a framework for customization, allowing individuals to tailor their dreams according to personal tastes and ideals. Sufficient financial resources ensure a stress-free retirement, prioritizing health and fitness enhances overall happiness, and a willingness to welcome new experiences fosters feelings of satisfaction.

Importance of Setting New Goals in Retirement

Setting new life objectives in retirement: Retirement is not only a means of coming to an end but rather a chance to start over and create a gratifying life. Setting new goals is essential for personal growth and a deep feeling of accomplishment in retirement. Let's examine the importance of this stage and compile advice for setting meaningful goals:

Sustaining purpose: Having goals gives post-career individuals focus and a strong feeling of motivation. By establishing fresh objectives, retirees may ensure they always maintain meaning and satisfaction in life, enhancing their post-career experience.

Personal growth: Taking up new activities and interests promotes continuous personal development. Retirement is a chance for ongoing self-improvement, enabling people to develop and discover facets of themselves that would have gone unnoticed throughout their working years.

Emotional well-being: Achieving new goals in retirement enhances emotional well-being and leaves a long-lasting feeling of achievement. Goal-setting and achievement foster an excellent emotional state, which enhances general well-being throughout the post-career period.

Social engagement: A thriving social life and new connections may result from following objectives and hobbies. Engaging in happy activities may foster deep relationships and guarantee a socially engaged and rewarding retirement.

When reaching retirement age, you are at a dynamic stage of life in which both new and old goals may improve. Those who put their health and well-being, travel, adventure, and financial security first throughout their retirement years may provide the groundwork for a successful retirement. At the same time, setting new objectives ensures that retirees will live contented lives, encouraging social interaction, personal growth, and emotional stability throughout this period of transition.

WAYS TO MAKE NEW OBJECTIVES IN RETIREMENT

Starting the retirement journey is not just about saying goodbye to work; it is an opportunity to create a gratifying and rewarding next phase of life. This guide explores meaningful ways to develop new goals, ensuring the post-career chapter is filled with ambitious pursuits and experiences.

Reflect on Passions: Rediscovering Enjoyable Pursuits

Consider Your Passions: During retirement, take the time to explore hobbies and interests that have always brought happiness and gratification. Discover interests or hobbies that may have been put on hold during your working years and reignite the joy they once brought.

Identify Areas for Personal Growth: Learning never stops. Look for opportunities to further education and personal development, setting goals that challenge and expand your knowledge and skills. Embrace the journey of continuous learning, enhancing your retirement life with intellectual stimulation.

Cultivate Relationships: Pursue shared interests to forge new connections and strengthen existing ones. Join classes, organizations, or groups that align with retirement goals, creating a vibrant social network that enriches your newfound freedom.

Embrace Adventure: Take advantage of retirement's newfound independence by planning trips and experiences that follow your passions. Explore places you have always dreamed of visiting, infusing post-career life with the excitement of adventure and discovery.

Contribute to Causes: Engage in meaningful volunteer work that resonates with your interests. Be a positive force in the community and support significant issues, leaving a lasting impact and contribution during retirement years.

Goal-Setting Techniques to Consider

- **Setting Great Goals:** Develop precise objectives using the smart framework (Doran, 1981):
- **Specific:** Clearly articulate goals.
- **Measurable:** Set benchmarks to track progress.
- **Achievable:** Ensure goals are realistic and attainable.
- **Relevant:** Align goals with values and aspirations. **Time-bound:**
- Establish deadlines to create structure and a sense of accomplishment.
- **Visualization:** Utilize the power of visualization to make goals feel more natural, immerse yourself mentally in achieving goals, and translate these visions into tangible representations in journals or vision boards.
- **Break Tasks Down:** For more complex goals, break them down into smaller, manageable tasks. Keeping things simple and focused will prevent feeling overwhelmed and allow steady progress without unnecessary stress. **Prioritize:** Determine priorities for goals based on current needs and personal values. Focus on the most relevant objectives and ensure efforts are directed towards

what matters the most, leading to a more impactful and complete retirement journey.

Establishing new goals in retirement is a powerful way to shape the next phase of life. By embracing new pursuits and engaging in activities that bring joy and fulfillment, retirees can create an enriching and purpose-driven post-career existence. Retirement can become a canvas waiting to be filled with intention and achievement.

A Journey Towards Retirement Success: A Comprehensive Guide to Effective Goal-Setting

Viewing it as more than just a destination is essential when preparing for retirement. It is about creating a satisfying and enjoyable journey. Setting goals for this significant phase requires careful thought and planning. This guide provides valuable insights into establishing achievable and meaningful goals in retirement.

- **Be Specific:** Clarity is vital when aiming for a rewarding retirement. Instead of settling for vague aspirations like "travel more," be precise about the places and activities that genuinely resonate with your desires. Setting specific goals creates a roadmap for retirement adventures. **Set Realistic Goals:** Ground aspirations in reality by appraising the feasibility of objectives. Give thought to factors such as time constraints, financial situation, and overall health. Realistic goals align with resources and limitations, ensuring retirement dreams remain within reach.
- **Create a Timeline:** Setting deadlines can help structure retirement aspirations. Time-bound objectives provide motivation and focus. For more ambitious goals, break them down into smaller, manageable activities with specific timeframes. This way, you can monitor progress and stay on track.

- **Review and Adjust:** The journey to retirement is everchanging, so you should periodically evaluate your goals. Stay adaptable and be open to making course corrections as needed. Regularly reviewing and adjusting goals will ensure they stay relevant and attainable throughout the retirement journey.

- **Visualize Your Success:** Immerse yourself in the vision of success for each goal set. Visualization not only enhances commitment but also motivates you to keep going. Envisioning the realization of objectives can boost determination and help you stay focused on the journey ahead.

- **Prioritize Your Goals:** With so many retirement aspirations, it is necessary to identify the most significant ones. Prioritize objectives based on values, ensuring focus on a manageable number. Having a limited number of critical goals will prevent becoming overwhelmed and assist in achieving them.

- **Seek Support:** Share retirement plans with loved ones, friends, or a mentor. Building a support network encourages accountability and provides a collective celebration of successes. The journey becomes even more satisfying in the company of those who matter. • **Balance Long-Term and Short-Term Goals:** Striking a balance between immediate and long-term goals is vital for progress. Mix easily achievable goals with those that require more time and effort. This balanced approach ensures a continuous feeling of accomplishment throughout retirement.

- **Be Adaptable:** Life after retirement may bring unexpected changes. Embrace adaptability and be open to modifying goals when necessary. Being flexible allows you to navigate the uncertainties of retirement with resilience and grace. • **Celebrate Milestones:** As you pursue goals, celebrate achievements along the way. Acknowledge and commemorate milestones as they occur. Celebrations provide motivation and reinforce positive behavior, making the retirement journey more enjoyable and rewarding.

These pointers will help create goals to better prepare for the thrilling and life-changing retirement experience. Every objective serves as a springboard for a fruitful and meaningful life after work.

Comprehensive Guide to Budgeting Before and After Retirement

Welcome to your one-stop resource for learning the art of budgeting and controlling retirement funds. This extensive guide will help you comprehend the importance of budgeting and provide step-by-step instructions, practical advice, and real-world solutions to guarantee a financially secure retirement.

Embarking on the journey toward retirement requires a clear understanding of your financial landscape. Budgeting is important and serves as a guide to navigating the complexities of pre and post-retirement finances.

Be honest about your financial situation: It is crucial to be honest about your financial standing before entering the golden years. Creating a pre-retirement budget will help you understand finances better. Triton Financial Group stresses the importance of this step.

Acknowledge reality: The first step towards smart planning is accepting your current financial standing. Look at spending habits, find areas where you can save without sacrificing your lifestyle, and set realistic savings goals based on your income before retirement. Investopedia suggests seeking advice from financial professionals for a personalized approach.

How to create a budget - Pre-retirement planning: Creating a budget involves multiple steps. Start by tracking earnings, setting clear objectives, and monitoring expenses. Separate costs into necessities and wants and a portion for savings and investments, using spreadsheets to track spending. Regularly adjust your budget in response to changes in income or expenses to stay financially prepared.

After Retirement: Maintaining Your Financial Stability

Stay on track: Moving from pre-retirement to post-retirement requires adjusting your budget. Evaluate spending habits, align them with priorities and new lifestyle, create an emergency fund for unexpected expenses, and regularly review and update your budget to meet evolving needs.

How to create a budget - post-retirement execution: Implementing a solid budget after retirement involves taking action. Set up automatic deposits into savings and investment accounts, use budgeting apps or online tools to monitor monthly expenses, and thoroughly review your budget every three months. Fidelity suggests making adjustments as needed and seeking professional advice for significant financial changes.

Comprehensive guide: CNBC offers a detailed guide that walks through the entire budgeting process, highlighting the nuances of post-retirement budgeting. This guide covers assessing retirement income sources, creating a monthly budget that includes expected expenses, accounting for long-term care and healthcare costs, and developing a plan for managing debt during retirement.

Successful retirement planning relies on meticulous budgeting. Each step is a strategic move toward financial security and achieving retirement goals, from pre-retirement preparation to executing a post-retirement budget. These comprehensive guidelines provide the tools to navigate the complex financial landscape at every stage of your retirement journey.

TIPS FOR BUDGETING

Regarding budgeting, several helpful resources provide information and practical advice to maximize funds. For instance, Securian Financial emphasizes setting spending priorities, particularly for necessities like food, shelter, and utilities. They advise adopting modest living habits and budgeting for medical expenses to make your money go further.

Nationwide (n.d) provides a list of practical elements that may successfully direct your financial planning efforts. These include evaluating home modifications, such as downsizing to save money, monitoring your budget regularly, and maximizing retirement income techniques, such as Social Security preparation.

Yahoo Finance (n.d.) offers various methods for saving money without sacrificing quality of life. They advise looking into loyalty programs for discounts, canceling unwanted subscription services, and examining insurance plans for possible savings. To augment retirement income, they also advise considering part-time or freelance employment (Nationwide, n.d.).

Senior Lifestyle (n.d) provides comprehensive financial management advice catered exclusively to seniors. They provide 27 valuable suggestions to optimize savings, such as keeping a close eye on monthly spending, using community services and senior discounts, and emphasizing meal preparation and energy-efficient house improvements as efficient strategies to save costs in retirement (Nationwide, n.d.).

Budgeting is not a one-size-fits-all process. Customizing financial planning for retirement is the key to success. Instead of just setting a budget, follow these thorough instructions, realistic ideas, and beneficial advice to construct a blueprint for retirement financial success.

Think About Reducing: Look into moving or downsizing to lower overall living expenses.

Advice from Financial Advisors: Consult a financial counselor for advice on customizing your plan to meet retirement objectives.

Here are 4 of Investopedia's 10 Recommendations for Secure Retirement

All-inclusive Retirement Scheme: Create a thorough retirement plan that includes recurring spending and future medical costs.

Examine Part-Time Employment: Contemplate part-time employment to preserve financial stability and augment retirement income.

Constant Evaluation of Portfolio: Regularly review and modify your investment portfolio to meet evolving requirements.

Assistance for Financial Advisors: Consult a financial professional for tailored advice on your retirement path.

TowneBank's Working in Retirement: What You Need to Know

Benefits to the Individual and the Budget: Recognize the advantages of part-time employment for one's financial and personal well-being.

Mental and Emotional Well-being: Recognize that working parttime positively impacts emotional and mental well-being.

Examine Flexible Work Schedules: Investigate flexible employment opportunities that complement your abilities and interests.

Valuable Income Stream: Acknowledge part-time employment as a useful source of income, particularly for paying off outstanding debt.

These thorough instructions cover everything from investing to budgeting to the possible advantages of part-time employment, offering a complete approach to reaching financial stability in retirement.

Managing Retirement's Financial Stability and Security: A comprehensive approach

The path to post-professional financial well-being involves distinguishing between financial stability and security. This guide aims to examine the nuances of these ideas, emphasize the significance of financial stability, break down the elements of a financially secure retirement, and provide practical guidance for long-term financial well-being.

Evaluating and contrasting financial security and stability: Are they equivalent? It is critical to comprehend the distinctions between stability and financial security. This section explores how these concepts work together to provide a solid financial foundation.

The value of having financial security: Protect your wealth and the importance of having a sound financial situation. This section examines how having enough money shields people from unanticipated challenges and uncertainties and positively impacts overall health. Components of a financially secure retirement include:

Savings and investing: Build a diversified portfolio to protect future financial security. Allocate funds in a manner that advances retirement goals.

Emergency fund: Set aside a sizable amount of money for unforeseen expenses.

Debt management: Establish priorities and deal with any unpaid bills efficiently.

Insurance coverage: Ensure you have full coverage, including health and long-term care.

Tips to Achieve Financial Security

Here are Four Preventive steps to ensure financially durable stability:

Establish a reasonable budget: Create a budget that accounts for your desired lifestyle and retirement. Give necessary costs priority while still making time for fun and relaxation.

Continuous learning and adjustment: Keep up with market developments and modify your plan as necessary.

Explore part-time employment: To maintain financial security and supplement income, reflect on part-time work.

Regular financial check-ups: Regularly evaluate and revise your financial plan to account for changes in circumstances.

When navigating the realms of stability and financial security, it is essential to adopt a holistic perspective. These tools and helpful advice function as a compass, guiding you toward a stable, secure, and resilient retirement.

Setting Out on a Lifetime Adventure: Making Your Dream Retirement Bucket List

Retirement, defined as the cessation of job duties, offers a fantastic chance for personal development, discovery, and satisfaction that goes beyond financial security. In this perspective, retirement bucket lists are intriguing because they enable people to articulate their goals and ambitions for this era in their lives. This section delves deeply into retirement bucket lists, evaluating their meaning, value, and creative possibilities:

- **The purpose of a bucket list:** When we carefully examine the advantages of making a retirement bucket list, we discover that it catalyzes improved desire and the pursuit of long-term goals regardless of age or condition. Exploring the psychological and emotional basis of this undertaking has several benefits, including developing enthusiasm and determination while cultivating a strong feeling of achievement and success.

- **Fantastic reasons to create a bucket list:** When we analyze the several compelling reasons for creating a retirement bucket list, we find a variety of justifications that indicate its ability to strengthen relationships, increase general well-being, and fill life with newfound vigor and resolve. The retirement bucket list, guided by self-fulfillment and personal progress, serves as a tool for transforming ambitions into practical milestones that move people toward a meaningful and rewarding existence.

- **There are several benefits of using a to-do list:** Creating a retirement bucket list requires a mix of introspection and practicality, emphasizing the significance of matching objectives with personal beliefs and interests. However, it is also a journey full of hope and possibilities, with each item on the list serving as a testimony to one's desires and goals.

- **Bucket list journey—The process of creating a list:** Creating a retirement bucket list requires a methodical strategy that includes self-reflection, desire, and adaptation. It entails a dynamic interaction of changing interests and objectives, culminating in an inspirational blueprint for a purpose-driven retirement.

- **Retirement bucket list ideas:** Retirement bucket list inspiration may be obtained in various places for a broad range of experiences to bring color and pleasure to their retirement. From cultural pursuits to adventurous experiences, the opportunities are as limitless as the imagination.

Finally, building a retirement bucket list is more than just a desire; it is a profound journey of self-discovery, satisfaction, and meaning. It highlights the human spirit's limitless ability for development and discovery, providing a road map to a retirement full of vitality, determination, and adventure.

Worksheet for Retirement Budget is an Interactive Element **Budgeting**

for Your Retirement:

- Make use of the components of the retirement budget spreadsheets that are available via the links below. Worksheet on
- Retirement Budget for the University of Oregon: https://hr.uoregon.edu/content/retirementbudget-worksheet
- Worksheets for TIAA Retirement Expense and Income: https://www.tiaa.org/public/pdf/r/retirement_expenseincome_worksheets.pdf
- Retire Well Budget Calculator: Compile earnings, outlays, and savings to produce thorough pre- and post-retirement budgets.: https://www.retirewell.com.au/files/ budget_planner.pdf

Set off on this journey with the information needed to approach retirement with purpose, excitement, and prudent money management. Everything on your bucket list awaits, along with your dream retirement!

As we approach retirement, it is time to examine the dynamics of self-discovery and personal pleasure. Salutations from the "Me" and "I" after retirement in Chapter Three. In this new phase of life, be ready to learn more about yourself and enjoy the joys of selfdiscovery once again.

THE "ME" AND "I" IN RETIREMENT

"Retirement is a blank sheet of paper. It is a chance to redesign your life into something new and different."

— PATRICK FOLEY

TRANSFORMATIVE MAGIC HOBBIES

Finding pleasure via meaningful activities reveals a world where hobbies become powerful health supplements. This story explores the health benefits of focused hobbies and how they may change a life.

The health benefits of having a hobby: Introspective journeys show how hobbies improve well-being. Dr. Serenity Guru promotes hobbies such as passports for peace and stress reduction. People find peace in life's chaos by engaging in relaxing hobbies (Hickling, 2022).

Mental agility improvement: Joy Weaver, a psychologist, says hobbies improve mental clarity and creativity. While pursuing their interests, people develop their cognitive abilities and spark new ideas.

Enhancing mental agility: Explore the well-being developed by hobbies to discover how meaningful activities improve stress management and body-mind harmony. According to the Calm Lifestyle Guardian (n.d.), hobbies provide comfort and stability throughout life's storms. By incorporating these activities into everyday routines, people build resilience and inner serenity despite outward turbulence.

How having a hobby benefits your health: The Neurologist Wellness Maestro explains how hobbies improve the mind and body beyond brain stimulation. Through deliberate activity, people achieve a physical and mental balance that exceeds established health paradigms.

Mental health benefits of hobbies: By exploring the mental health advantages of hobbies, people find the transformational power of deliberate getaways and proud moments. The Mental Wellness Trailblazer praises hobbies as thoughtful escapes from contemporary life pressures. Honoring accomplishments fosters self-worth and a grateful outlook (Parkhurst, 2021).

Body-mind harmony: When people look at the advantages of hobbies, they find unexpected connections between cardiovascular health and community relationships built through shared interests. The Cardiologist Heart Maven urges individuals to let their hearts dance to their hobbies since they know the substantial health advantages of engaging in activities that bring them pleasure. The Sociologist Connection Maven places a great emphasis on the significance of hobbies in the process of establishing solid relationships and a sense of community among people who have similar interests.

As individuals embark on their hobby adventures, they profoundly influence these pursuits on their overall well-being. Beyond mere activities, hobbies weave threads of happiness, fortitude, and contentment into the fabric of life, enriching each moment with enthusiasm and vitality (Venkat, 2022).

Identifying Your Ideal Interest

Embark on a journey of discovery as retirement unfolds, not just as another chapter but as a vast expedition into interests and passions. Let's navigate through the possibilities, uncovering the treasures that await within. The journey is the goal, and each step leads closer to self-discovery. Exploration nurtures interests in retirement, so follow your curiosity.

How to discover interests after retirement:

1. Take the time to reflect on past passions and experiences.
2. Explore the echoes of what once was exciting, as they may hold the dormant seeds of hobbies waiting to be rediscovered.
3. Engage in social interactions, as chance encounters can reveal hidden interests. Connecting with others can open doors to new avenues of exploration.

Tips for finding a hobby in retirement:

1. Try out various activities until finding the one that ignites your soul.
2. Treat the search for hobbies like a culinary adventure, exploring with enthusiasm until you discover your favorite flavor.
3. Revisit the dreams of youth, as nostalgia can often be the guide towards timeless passions.

How to find new hobbies and interests in retirement:

1. Embrace curiosity as your guide, leading into uncharted territories of exploration.
2. Ask questions and embrace the unknown, as that is where discovery lies.
3. Look for common threads in past hobbies, which can lead to new horizons and desires.

Recreation and social engagement —discovering new interests during retirement: Immerse yourself in recreation and social engagement while navigating retirement. The interplay of leisure and camaraderie will be the magic of novelty. Forge connections and explore new paths in the pursuit of contentment.

Advice to Help You Navigate the World of Leisure

Explore the beautiful fabric of communal life, where similar interests weave neighbors together in a brilliant mosaic.

Community canvas: Explore local associations where shared interests and aspirations drive community life. Find interests and kindred spirits who brighten the days in the busy streets of community involvement.

Study without boundaries: Learn without boundaries and embrace lifelong learning, where each day is a new chapter in the journey of discovery. Immerse yourself in the vast expanse of knowledge like an everlasting student because enlightenment is the genuine essence of life.

Take up a retirement interest: Pursue new hobbies with intent and curiosity.

Start small, dream big: Plant curiosity in the rich soil of dreams and watch them grow. As a gardener tends to fragile petals, patiently and diligently grow your interests.

Embrace the unknown: Explore unfamiliar paths to unearth hidden riches. In unknown territory, the unusual may lie in the shadows, promising discovery and amazement.

Taking Off with a Novel Interest: An Entire Range of Options

Retirement starts a new chapter filled with colorful activities just waiting to be explored; it's not the end of the adventure. This varied selection of 50 odd and distinctive pastime suggestions is designed for this thrilling stage of life.

Creative activities: Welcome to art, where imagination rules and creativity is limitless. Express yourself through crafts and performances and weave your story into life.

Mosaic magic: Use mosaic tiles to create stunning art that inspires the senses and imagination. Create elaborate artworks that express volumes without words by assembling brilliant colors and textures.

Paper quilling: Enjoy paper quilling, a delicate technique that transforms strips of paper into complex designs that captivate the eye and calm the spirit. With each roll and twist, ordinary paper becomes a canvas for endless imagination.

Wood carving: Indulge in the timeless art of wood carving, where talented hands personalize timber blocks with tales and aspirations. Feel the wood texture under your hands while constructing beautiful sculptures that highlight your skill.

Glassblowing: Discover the captivating world of glassblowing, where molten glass transforms into stunning sculptures under expert supervision beneath flickering flames. Discover the magic of fire and glass, shaping liquid crystals into stunning sculptures.

Eco-friendly crafting: For eco-friendly crafting, use wasted materials to create beautiful art that promotes environmental awareness. Turn garbage into treasure and make a statement with art using ingenuity.

Artistic performances - Improvisational theatre: Experience the spontaneity and inventiveness of improvisational theater in artistic performances. Think quickly, be witty, and enjoy spontaneous storytelling that captivates.

Street performing: Use the streets as a platform to showcase your passion via engaging performances that blend art and reality. Showcase abilities outside, enlightening passersby with your charm.

Storytelling: Use storytelling to engage listeners with powerful narratives and beautiful language. Bring people and worlds to life with each word, preserving storytelling for future generations.

Literary exploration: Explore literature and use words to create captivating stories that inspire the spirit. If you write haiku poetry, memoirs, or bookbinding, let the words resonate through time and shape the human experience.

Musical marvels: Explore a variety of engaging activities to express yourself. Each activity, from musical instruments to outdoor activities, will fire enthusiasm and nurture the spirit.

Harmonica tone: Take the harmonica and produce soul-stirring tunes that touch your soul. Give the notes life with each breath, and allow the music to carry you to a peaceful and joyful place.

Drumming ethnically: Explore ancient civilizations via drumming. Connect with rhythm, overcome borders, and embrace cultural variety to feel the world's pulse in your spirit.

Ukulele serenade: With its lovely tunes, the ukulele will take you on a musical trip. Enjoy musical expression as you strum away the day's worries and immerse yourself in captivating sounds.

Fitness and sports: Experience the exhilaration of outdoor activities, each challenging you to try new things. Whether paddleboarding, archery, or rock climbing, each activity stimulates the senses and revitalizes your soul.

Tech-savvy explorations: Explore the digital world's endless potential with cutting-edge technology. Each technology endeavor promises to broaden horizons and change your reality, from unmanned aerial photography to virtual reality excursions.

Culinary adventures: Explore the rich tapestry of tastes and smells from around the world on a culinary adventure that feeds the spirit. Each culinary adventure promises to satisfy your curiosity and joy, from improving your cooking abilities and trying new cuisines to learning about fermentation and food review blogging.

Nature-inspired activities: Explore and appreciate nature's beauties. Each nature-based activity, whether birdwatching, botanical illustration, or beekeeping, will deepen your connection with the world.

Mindful, relaxing hobbies: Mindful activities that calm the soul and spirit promote inner serenity. Whether practicing Tai Chi, Zen gardening, or yoga, any mindful activity will calm the mind, relax your body, and restore equilibrium.

Social and community activities: Help others and make a difference in the community. Each activity, whether working for a cause you care about or community-building, will form relationships and improve the world.

Explore and find yourself. May each activity kindle passion and nurture your spirit, enhancing your life beyond measure.

General Outdoor Safety Tips for Seniors

Getting outside may be a refreshing experience, particularly for older adults. However, planning for various things, such as season specific conditions and basic safety procedures, is necessary to ensure a fun and safe outdoor excursion. Let's examine some priceless counsel, including general recommendations and guidance specific to certain times of the year.

Buddy System Happiness: Enjoy the pleasure of company by going on outdoor activities whenever possible with a friend, neighbor, or relative. This adds a degree of security and improves safety standards, as well as the experience.

Comfortable steps: Prioritize supportive and cozy footwear to preserve stability and lower the chance of falling. The seemingly simple choice to wear suitable footwear may significantly impact safety while negotiating outdoor terrain.

Stay alert and attentive: Be mindful of surroundings, particularly while crossing roadways. Reduce outside distractions and maintain awareness of surroundings so you can always move cautiously and mindfully.

Seasonal style: Make sure clothing fits the current weather. In the summer, use breathable materials to provide comfort and protection from harsh temperatures, and in the winter, layer garments to remain warm.

Hydration station: Always carry a bottle of water to stay hydrated. Maintaining enough hydration is crucial for general health and a primary safety measure while engaging in outdoor sports.

Sunshine smarts: Use preventative care outside in the sun to prevent damaging UV rays. For additional protection and style, don a wide-brimmed hat and apply sunscreen.

Recognize your boundaries: Listen to the body's signals and know when to stop doing something or take a break if you feel uncomfortable or tired. Exceeding your boundaries may jeopardize security.

Emergency essentials: Make sure your mobile phone is fully charged and always have a list of emergency contacts. These necessities come in handy in an emergency, providing comfort and quick access to help. **Seasonal Guidance:**

A wonderland in the winter - Warm heart, warm layers: When venturing out on frigid winter evenings, dress in layers to be warm. Remember your hat and gloves to protect extremities from frostbite.

Watch your step: Take care while walking on ice surfaces, and consider wearing non-slip footwear for better grip and stability.

Limit exposure: Reduce outside activity during very low temperatures to avoid the harmful effects of extended exposure to cold weather on the body.

Summer glow: First Lights Benefit: To escape the oppressive noon heat, make the most of the cooler early hours for outdoor activities.

Staying hydrated: Drink enough water regularly to combat the summer heat and avoid dehydration.

Comfortable cooling: To avoid overheating in the summer, use light clothes, caps, and umbrellas to protect from the sun's rays.

Let's Get Crafty: 10 Meaningful Crafts for You and Your Loved Ones

Crafting is more than simply making lovely things; it is a means to express imagination and provide thoughtful presents for loved ones. Here are some simple but essential craft ideas that spark imagination:

Making unique presents allows you to show how much you care and express your creativity to loved ones, adding a unique touch to any event. Let's look at several senior-friendly crafting ideas that give different chances for personalization and ingenuity.

Customized cards for greetings (Excellent Senior Living): To make custom greeting cards, gather colorful paper, markers, glue, scissors, and embellishments. To give birthdays, holidays, and other special occasions a unique touch, combine vibrant colors, thought-provoking wording, and personalized decorations.

Beaded bracelets (Amanda's Crafts): This craft requires a clasp, scissors, elastic cord, and beads. Choose beads of different sizes and hues to create lovely beaded bracelets. Stringing elastic rope and a clasp together can make unique presents for loved ones.

Hand-knit dishcloths (Courtyard Manor): Use cotton yarn and knitting needles to make colorful and useful hand-knit dishcloths.

These practical things may be made using easy knitting designs and are an excellent present for anybody who appreciates cooking.

Memory scrapbooks - An older adult's guide: To construct memory scrapbooks gather colored paper, stickers, glue, a scrapbook, and images. By organizing pictures, adding stickers, writing captions, and decorating with bright paper and stickers, create individualized mementos for priceless experiences.

Wooden toy designs (Amanda's Crafts): For this craft, assemble paint, brushes, sandpaper, and wood pieces. Paint and assemble wooden components to create a range of entertaining wooden toys, such as puzzles and small automobiles. These toys make lovely gifts for kids or grandkids.

Courtyard Manor's masterpiece birdhouse: Decorate a wooden birdhouse with paint, brushes, and other materials to create a comfortable sanctuary for feathery companions. Striking colors and patterns make it a beautiful and environmentally responsible addition to any outdoor area.

Picture frames with mosaics (SSWW): To construct beautiful mosaic picture frames, gather glue, mosaic tiles, and old photo frames. Attach colorful mosaic tiles to the frames to create eyecatching patterns and a personal touch with your most treasured pictures.

Embellished tote bags made of fabric (Amanda Crafts): Gather stencils, fabric paint, and plain tote bags to create stylish and distinctive tote bags ideal for shopping or transporting necessities.

Pressed flower bookmarks - A resource for seniors: This project will require heavy books, flowers, and laminating sheets. To preserve the beauty of flowers, make pressed flower bookmarks and laminate them to create presents that are both durable and inspired by nature.

Decorative glass jars (SSWW): Paint elaborate designs onto plain glass jars. Use glass jars, paint, and brushes to turn them into lovely decorative receptacles ideal for keeping little things or providing ornamental touches to any area.

A thrilling voyage awaits in Chapter Four, "Finding Your Forever Home." In this chapter, we will explore the search for the ideal haven where solace, happiness, and memories come together. Come along as we delve into the art of identifying the perfect home and/or country for this new phase of life.

FINDING YOUR FOREVER HOME

THE GLOBAL QUEST FOR THE PERFECT RETIREMENT HAVEN

As the sun sets on one chapter of our lives, the prospect of retirement opens doors to new horizons and possibilities. However, where in the world should one spend their golden years? Let's embark on a fascinating journey exploring the top countries that beckon retirees with promises of tranquility, adventure, and a comfortable lifestyle.

According to the insights from International Living, a renowned authority on expatriate living, the world is brimming with enticing retirement options (International Living, n.d.). The possibilities seem boundless, from Central America's lush landscapes to Europe's cultural richness.

In their latest rankings, Business Insider unveils the top ten countries offering not just retirement but a comfortable retirement (Business Insider, 2023). Imagine waking up to breathtaking vistas, indulging in local cuisines, and immersing yourself in diverse cultures while enjoying the peace of mind that comes with a wellplanned retirement.

Nevertheless, wait, the quest does not end there. US News & World Report has insights into the best countries to retire, offering a nuanced perspective that considers factors like healthcare, cost of living, and overall quality of life (US News, n.d.). As we delve into the top-ranking nations, discover that retirement is not just a phase but an opportunity to curate the life you always dreamed of.

So, fasten your seatbelts for this exhilarating exploration of the top countries for retirement. Whether seeking the serenity of coastal paradises, the charm of historic cities, or the adventure of uncharted territories, our journey begins.

Moving After Retirement: Weighing the Pros and Cons

Traveling to a new place in retirement presents various factors, each with pros and cons. Let's examine the many viewpoints provided by moving services and discuss the possible advantages and disadvantages of each.

Shift Moving: Moves bring fresh starts, a higher cost of living, and health advantages. For retirees, moving creates an opportunity for fresh starts by promoting travel, social interaction, and involvement in various activities. Certain regions have a more reasonable cost of living, allowing retirees to extend their retirement funds and preserve their financial security. For retirees, having access to better medical facilities and a more comfortable setting may enhance health results.

Potential difficulties: Leaving behind comfortable surroundings may cause emotional challenges and a feeling of loss, particularly for those well-ingrained in their communities. Social media and financial ramifications will be critical topics. Relocating involves significant costs, such as moving expenses and home transactions, which may often burden seniors' finances. Building new social networks may take some time, resulting in feelings of isolation and loneliness at first.

My Moving Reviews: Downsizing chances, exploration and adventure, and personalized living areas are the benefits of this move. Retirees who move after retirement downsize, often allowing them to live a simpler lifestyle and better use their living space. Retirees' cravings for adventure and excitement during their golden years might be satisfied by traveling to new locations and immersing themselves in other cultures. Retirees may customize their living environment to their tastes by selecting a home that satisfies their present and future demands.

The main obstacles are the market's volatility, friends and family, and the transition time. When one is separated from close friends and family, feelings of loneliness and a need for company arise. It may take time and effort to become used to a new environment, local traditions, and conveniences, leading to early pain and confusion. Unpredictability in real estate transactions may result in unanticipated difficulties or hold-ups in purchasing or selling a house.

Ensure Shift: Less responsibility and respect for the environment are two benefits of relocating to a region with a more temperate climate. Relocation to a more temperate environment may also improve seniors' quality of life and well-being in general. Retirees might have more free time and pursue personal interests when they live in a smaller house or neighborhood since there are frequently fewer maintenance duties to take care of.

Community integration and health access are corresponding issues. As retirees age, access to high-quality healthcare becomes more crucial, and regional differences in healthcare facilities may create difficulties. It may be challenging to integrate into a new community, particularly one with a well-established social structure, and it will require initiative to make relationships.

Royal Moving Company: Opportunities for culture and a change of environment are well-known advantages of relocating. Relocating exposes seniors to diverse cultural events and activities, promoting personal development and intellectual stimulation. Experiencing novel surroundings may stimulate the mind and soul, providing a revitalized feeling of direction and energy.

Notable challenges include regret and nostalgia, as well as logistical challenges. Older adults may find the physical and psychological strain of packing, moving, and unpacking items to be very high, which presents practical difficulties. Thinking back on former events and recollections may impact the general well-being of retirees during the transition phase, which may cause sentiments of regret or nostalgia.

Things to Consider When Making Your Decision

Embarking on a relocation journey after retirement necessitates assessing factors for a smooth transition. Let's explore the insights provided by reputable sources in the financial and advisory domains, shedding light on essential considerations for retirees contemplating a move.

Satori wealth - *Financial implications and access to healthcare:*

1. *Delve* into the financial ramifications of relocation, including taxes, housing costs, and overall living expenses.
2. Consult your financial advisor to ensure cohesive long-term financial objectives.
3. Thoroughly examine local healthcare options and proximity to medical providers to ensure continued access to essential healthcare services.

Great Oak Advisors - *Plan with emotional readiness:*

1. Mitigate stress associated with relocation by initiating preparation well in advance.
2. Address practical aspects such as hiring movers and downsizing possessions to streamline the moving process.
3. Mentally prepare for the transition by acknowledging potential challenges and embracing the opportunities for personal growth and adaptation.

US News – Finance - *Research potential locations and legal and tax considerations:* Conduct thorough research on prospective relocation destinations, reviewing factors such as climate, amenities, and available services to identify the most suitable environment. Know any legal and tax implications associated with relocating to a different state or country, ensuring compliance with relevant regulations and minimizing potential financial burdens.

The Motley Fool - *Social and community life and long-term vision:*

1. Evaluate the social opportunities offered by prospective retirement communities, ensuring alignment with personal interests and preferences.
2. Explore avenues for building social networks through community involvement and participation in local groups.
3. Align the chosen retirement community with long-term objectives and aspirations, ensuring it provides the necessary support and amenities to facilitate a gratifying retirement lifestyle.

Relocating after retirement demands careful consideration of various factors encompassing financial, healthcare, emotional, and social dimensions. By diligently preparing and researching potential destinations, retirees can embark on a relocation journey that aligns with their overarching retirement goals and enhances their overall well-being.

Signs or Indications of Upsizing Following Retirement:

To guarantee a smooth transition, carefully evaluate several variables before starting the process of downsizing your living area. Let us examine information from reliable financial and real estate sources to highlight important factors to think about when contemplating downsizing.

Brightland Homes—Transitioning lifestyle: Consider how your lifestyle has changed and whether your present home still suits requirements. If tastes have changed—perhaps you want to host more guests or take up new hobbies—give thought to simplifying.

Guest accommodations: Evaluate whether your current residence can comfortably host visiting friends and family. Also, assess how often you welcome visitors and whether more bedrooms or guest suites are needed.

Requirements for storage: To address storage issues, investigate downsizing solutions that provide more storage space. Ponder ways of downsizing may help you arrange belongings and make your home clutter-free.

The Motley Fool - Increased enjoyment and comfort: If wanting a cozier or more abundant living space, consider downsizing. Compare the financial effects of downsizing with the possible improvements in comfort and satisfaction.

House as an investment: When determining whether to improve, reflect on the market's state and assess your house as an investment. Before making a choice, evaluate the status of the real estate market and the possible return on investment.

Hobbies: Review whether downsizing can accommodate new interests or hobbies with dedicated places. Think about how downsizing could complement a changing lifestyle and provide room for certain places required for pastimes or interests.

LJ Hooker - Budget and affordability: Assess your financial situation to make sure that the reduction fits within your spending plan. Examine not only the new home's purchase price but also utilities and maintenance expenses.

Future prerequisites: Estimate future demands and determine if a larger home will suit any changes in your way of life. Think about how well the new property will accommodate future family size adjustments or lifestyle choices.

Situation of the market: Investigate the local real estate market to gain insight into elements like property appreciation and resale value. Examine the new property's position relative to other amenities, medical facilities, social infrastructure, airports, cruise ports, etc.

Downsizing plan: If you are moving to a bigger house to accommodate your evolving demands, create a downsizing plan to make the most of the available space. Ensure the new space efficiently complements your desired way of living.

In conclusion, downsizing after retirement may be a calculated move depending on shifting lifestyle demands and choices. Before making such a big move, it is crucial to thoroughly evaluate the indicators that point to the need for a bigger house and take into account several considerations. For a seamless transition and long-term decision satisfaction, it is essential to consider market circumstances, future demands, and financial factors.

Things to Take into Account While Making a Decision

Downsizing your living space requires careful consideration of financial, lifestyle, and emotional concerns. Let's examine the advice of respected financial and retirement planning sources on downsizing.

Financial implications: Assess your financial situation and how downsizing may affect your retirement, living expenditures, and financial security. Reflect on how a smaller house could affect your budget and long-term financial objectives.

Lifestyle goals:

1. Plan your downsizing around your living goals.
2. Consider changes in social interests, mobility, and healthy while choosing a new house.
3. Make sure your downsizing option matches your changing lifestyle goals.

Retirement ACTS: Assess your home's upkeep needs and how downsizing may reduce them. Give thought to relocating to a smaller, easier-to-maintain house to enjoy retirement with peace of mind.

Accessibility: Evaluate your home's stairs, layout, and design. Downsizing may improve your quality of life and long-term mobility.

Location and cost of living:

1. On Smart Asset, compare your present location to prospective downsizing areas.
2. Consider how relocating may affect finances and expenditures.
3. Select a location that fits the budget and offers the services you need.

Reflect on your emotional attachment to your house and things. Expect to let go of beloved items while downsizing and prepare mentally. Ask close ones for help.

MoneySmart - Government initiatives: Research reducing government programs and retiree cash incentives. Explore how to use these projects to downsize and improve your finances.

Downsizing may affect your eligibility for government pensions and other retirement benefits. To achieve a peaceful retirement, assess any income or financial changes from downsizing and prepare appropriately.

Signs You Need to Downsize:

Managing the process of reducing your house requires balancing mental and practical readiness. Let's explore the perspectives of reliable real estate and property management sources, which give insightful advice on identifying the signals when it is time to downsize and be ready for this significant change.

Household light: Find any unused spaces or rooms in your present house. Ponder how downsizing might result in a more effective and manageable living environment by optimizing space utilization and minimizing needless upkeep.

Financial strain: Finding it difficult to pay for the maintenance of your present home. To relieve financial pressure, think about reducing and repurchasing funds to live a more satisfying retirement.

Senior living: Physical limitations make it difficult to do basic housekeeping duties. Examine your possibilities for downsizing to find a more bearable living situation that fits your demands and present physical capabilities.

Your existing house has safety issues, such as stairwell difficulties. Make safety the priority and contemplate downsizing options that provide a safe and convenient living space.

Hampshire Villages - Modification Needs: Your present home is no longer suitable for your changing demands or way of life. If a smaller house better suits your needs, think about downsizing and making the necessary modifications to improve your living area.

Ways to prepare for a downsizing: Start sorting through and categorizing your possessions to decide what to give, sell, or retain. Consider downsizing as a chance to streamline your belongings and simplify your living area while concentrating on what brings you happiness and value.

Planning: Set up your renovated area thoughtfully to maximize utility and storage. Carefully think about where to put furniture and personal belongings to make the most of the available space and guarantee that every corner is used effectively.

The Spruce: Make a list of everything you own to prioritize goods for your new house and determine necessities. When you downsize, be sure the items you choose have meaning for you and will make your smaller living area more comfortable and happier.

Ask friends, family, or professionals for emotional assistance throughout the downsizing process. If you are going through a downsizing, surround yourself with a network of people who will be there to guide, encourage, and understand you through the emotional obstacles.

Tips and Mistakes to Avoid:

Reducing your house requires significant preparation and thinking before you begin to guarantee a successful transition. Let's examine the opinions of professionals in the fields of finance and retirement to learn more about essential things to explore and typical mistakes to avoid.

ACTS retirement – Make a plan: Give yourself enough time to plan the downsizing process and come to well-informed conclusions. Avoid making hasty judgments that you will later regret if you speed the reducing process.

Downsizing versus rightsizing: Give "rightsizing" more weight than just "downsizing" by choosing a place that fits your current requirements and way of life. If you just cut square footage without considering your unique needs, you may not be happy with your new living arrangement.

Investopedia - Neglecting the emotional effect: Investopedia recognizes and deals with the psychological effects of downsizing on your health, putting aside the fact that underestimating the emotional difficulties associated with downsizing might make the process more stressful and anxious.

Not considering future needs: When downsizing, contemplate future demands and any changes to your lifestyle or health. Review the need to make future improvements that might leave your smaller house unable to accommodate changing needs.

You may confidently handle the downsizing process and ensure that your new living arrangement fits your current lifestyle and future goals by paying attention to these insightful tips and avoiding frequent errors.

Retirement downsizing is a difficult choice that must be well thought out regarding lifestyle, finances, and emotions. Wasted space, mounting debt, upkeep challenges, and evolving demands might indicate a desire to reduce. Decluttering, organizing one's environment, and getting emotional support are all part of the downsizing preparation process. It's critical to prepare ahead of time, concentrate on "rightsizing," and avoid minimizing the emotional effect or ignoring requirements down the road. Retirees may make their golden years more bearable and satisfying by adequately handling the downsizing process.

Renting vs Buying: Making the Decision for Retirement

Whether to purchase or rent a property becomes more important as one approaches retirement and explores lifestyle and financial planning. Many variables are at play, and each has pros and cons. Let us examine the complexities of this choice and the expert viewpoints presented.

Pros and Cons: Let's dive deeper into the discussion of renting or buying a house to guide us on the way through this incredible journey:

Renting: Many retirees find that renting offers a certain amount of freedom. According to Investopedia, tenants can downsize or move places easily, and the landlord is responsible for all upkeep. The disadvantage is that there is no equity accumulation since rent only goes toward occupancies rather than ownership.

Purchasing: Owning a property is often seen as a long-term investment. Mortgage payments provide a feeling of security and control over the property as they accumulate equity. However, homeowners are accountable for upkeep and changes in the real estate market.

Additional Perspectives: Considering information from several sources, including US News (n.d.) and AARP (n.d.), renting is recommended due to its cheaper initial expenses and financial flexibility, but it also restricts customization and the possibility of rent rises. The security and long-term investment that owning a house offers are highly valued, but there are important factors to allow for, such as maintenance expenses and market fluctuations.

Additional Considerations for Decision-Making

In addition to the advantages and disadvantages, additional considerations are crucial in this decision-making process. According to SmartAsset, retirees should assess the state of the economy, including interest rates and property prices. As MoneySmart (n.d.) recommends, financial objectives and ideal retirement lifestyles should align with the selected course of action.

Noteworthy Hidden Expenses of Home Ownership

Despite its attraction, retirement income may be impacted by the hidden expenses of housing. ACTS Retirement cautions that property taxes, regular upkeep, and unforeseen repairs may add up over time. CNBC adds to the list, emphasizing prospective Homeowner Association (HOA) dues, homeowner's insurance, and monthly utilities as necessary continuing costs.

The upfront expenses of becoming a homeowner are highlighted by Investopedia, along with the opportunity cost of the down payment— money that might have been invested in other areas with the possibility of earning more money. Forbes also highlights the costs associated with renovations and house remodeling, which are often disregarded.

The decision to purchase or rent in the context of retirement life becomes complex and requires a careful analysis of one's longterm objectives, financial capabilities, and personal preferences. A comprehensive awareness of the ramifications will help seniors make this important decision and choose a living arrangement that fits their retirement path.

A Complete Guide to Exploring Retirement Communities

Seniors looking for a lively and encouraging place to live in their golden years are increasingly choosing retirement communities. Let's explore the nuances of retirement homes, how they operate, how they differ from assisted living, and the factors to consider when selecting one.

Retirement communities: What are they? Retirement communities are apartment buildings reserved for older adults that provide various services, facilities, and social events catered to their needs. These communities aim to provide a setting where people may live an active, self-sufficient lifestyle with access to various support services.

How do they operate? Retirement communities blend autonomous living with a range of amenities and services. Most residents live in their flats or houses inside the community, but they may also use food options, health initiatives, and social events. The communities often plan social activities, excursions, and educational opportunities to foster community among the members.

Assisted Living vs. Retirement Communities

While assisted living facilities and retirement communities provide services for older adults, their goals are distinct.

Retirement communities: Retirement communities prioritize independent living, offering a communal environment for elderly individuals to participate in social events and sustain an active way of life.

Assisted facilities: They improve the general quality of life by providing a range of facilities, including fitness centers, play areas, and shared meals.

Assisted Living - supportive care: Assisted living, in contrast, is designed for those who need help with everyday tasks or managing their medications.

Individualized care: Based on each resident's unique requirements, assisted living facilities create individualized care plans that guarantee residents get the assistance they need. It is salient to find out more about the distinctions between assisted living and retirement facilities:

Exploring Retirement Communities' Pros and Cons of Living

Socializing, facilities, security, and maintenance-free living are benefits. Retirement communities' built-in social network promotes companionship and reduces social isolation. Residents get access to eating and exercise facilities and cleaning, improving their quality of life and convenience. Safety and security are priorities in retirement communities, giving older persons and their families peace of mind. Residents may live maintenance-free since the community handles exterior maintenance.

Price, limited independence, and healthcare services are cons. Depending on location and amenities, retirement communities might be too expensive for some. Retirement homes are helpful, yet some members may find them confining, limiting their freedom and autonomy. Some retirement communities offer healthcare, but people with more complex requirements may need to move to assisted living or skilled nursing facilities, which may be difficult.

Retirees may decide whether retirement community living fits their lifestyle, finances, and long-term care requirements by carefully weighing these advantages and drawbacks.

HOW TO PICK THE IDEAL RETIREMENT COMMUNITY FOR YOU

Selecting the ideal retirement community requires giving much thought to one's requirements, interests, and way of life. Lumina provides a thoughtful analysis of this critical choice:

Location: When deciding on a location, allow for closeness to friends, family, and your favorite features.

Amenities and services: Check if the facilities and services align with your needs and tastes.

Cost and financial planning: Recognize all associated expenses, such as monthly dues, admission fees, and other possible expenditures.

Community culture: Understand the vibe and customs and see whether they suit your social tastes.

Medical support: Consider the community's degree of healthcare assistance and if it can accommodate your future demands.

To sum up, retirement communities provide seniors with an active living choice that encourages an independent yet supported lifestyle. Comprehending the differences between assisted living and retirement communities is essential, and weighing the benefits and drawbacks may help people make the best decision. When choosing a retirement community, a happy and pleasant retirement will result from careful attention to cost, community culture, facilities, location, and healthcare assistance.

Retiring Abroad: A Comprehensive Guide to Signs and Successful Relocation

Let's explore these guides to ensure problem-free relocation as retirees:

Deciding to retire abroad - Recognizing the signs: Retiring abroad is a significant life decision that opens doors to new experiences and opportunities. Understanding the signs indicating that you may be ready for such a move is crucial for a successful transition. Let us explore these signs based on insights from reputable sources:

Financial preparedness: According to a Yahoo Finance article, having a stable and fixed income that allows for a comfortable lifestyle abroad is a critical indicator. Before considering the move, individuals should assess their financial readiness and whether their income supports the desired lifestyle in a new country.

Adventurous spirit and openness: Escape Artist emphasizes the importance of being adventurous and open to embracing new cultures. The desire for exploration and a willingness to adapt to a different way of life indicate a mindset conducive to retiring abroad.

Desire for change: AARP points out that the yearning for change is a significant sign. If you are seeking new experiences and a different lifestyle in retirement, it may be time to consider the possibilities that retiring abroad can offer.

Global outlook: USA Today suggests that having an international outlook and being open to diverse perspectives are critical signs. Retiring abroad often involves navigating different cultural norms and practices, making a global mindset essential for a smooth transition.

Tips for a Successful Relocation: Planning, Financial Considerations, and Practical Advice

Once the decision to retire abroad is made, careful planning and practical considerations become paramount. Let's delve into expert advice from Forbes, Great Oak Advisors, PODS, and Real Simple to ensure a successful and stress-free relocation:

Early planning: Forbes stresses the importance of early planning. Initiating preparations well in advance allows individuals to address logistical and legal aspects efficiently. This includes obtaining necessary documents, understanding visa requirements, and planning the logistics of the move.

Financial understanding: Great Oak Advisors recommends a thorough understanding of the financial implications of the move. This involves considering tax implications and currency exchange rates and establishing a financial plan that aligns with the cost of living in the chosen destination.

Practical advice for a smooth move: PODS provides practical advice, including creating a detailed timeline for the move, researching local services at the destination, and decluttering before packing. These steps contribute to an organized and efficient relocation process.

Packing tips for efficiency: Real Simple's packing tips focus on organization and efficient use of space. From decluttering possessions to using proper packing materials, their advice aims to simplify the packing process and ensure that belongings arrive at the destination intact.

Additional Resources for a Stress-Free Move

In addition to the core tips, several resources offer comprehensive guides for a smooth transition:

Style at Home - Tips for an easy move: Style at Home provides a detailed guide with 21 tips for an easy, stress-free move. These encompass everything from packing strategies to organizing belongings effectively.

Moving - Top tips for a stress-free move: Moving's guide offers ten tips covering various aspects of the relocation process. From selecting a moving company to creating a moving checklist, their advice aims to alleviate stress during the move.

Moving.com - Moving tips and hacks: Moving.com presents a wealth of moving tips and hacks to simplify the moving experience. These include insights into packing efficiently, navigating the logistics, and ensuring a smooth transition to the new destination.

PODS Blog - Packing and moving tips: The PODS blog is a valuable resource for packing and moving tips. Its insights contribute to a well-organized and stress-free move and cover various aspects of the relocation process.

Constellation - Moving and packing checklist: Constellation's moving and packing checklist offers a comprehensive guide to staying organized during the move. From creating an inventory to managing utilities, this checklist ensures no detail is overlooked.

Embarking on an international retirement adventure is a journey filled with excitement and potential. By recognizing the signs, understanding the financial implications, and following expert advice, individuals can pave the way for a successful and fulfilling retirement abroad. These factors contribute to a seamless transition, allowing retirees to embrace new cultures and experiences in their chosen destinations.

The fifth chapter is "Retire, Roam, Rediscover... Repeat!" Get ready to embrace the spirit of adventure! This chapter takes us on an everlasting exploratory voyage filled with treasured memories and unexpected discoveries at every turn. Prepare to explore at leisure and rekindle your enthusiasm for life as we celebrate the pleasures of retirement travel.

MAKE A DIFFERENCE WITH YOUR REVIEW

UNLOCK THE POWER OF GENEROSITY

"The greatest gift you can give someone is your time, because when you give your time, you are giving a portion of your life that you will never get back."

— ANONYMOUS

People who give without expectation live longer, happier lives. So, if we've got a shot at that during our time together, let's make it happen.

To make that happen, I have a question for you...

Would you help someone you've never met, even if you never got credit for it?

Who is this person you ask? They are like you. Or, at least, like you used to be. Less experienced, wanting to make a difference, and needing help, but not sure where to look.

My mission is to make 'Retirement Beyond Finances' accessible to everyone. Everything I do stems from that mission. And the only way for me to accomplish that mission is by reaching... well...everyone.

This is where you come in. Most people do, in fact, judge a book by its cover (and its reviews). So, here's my ask on behalf of retirees you've never met:

Please help other retirees by leaving this book a review.

Your gift costs no money and less than 60 seconds to make real but can change a fellow retiree's life forever. Your review could help...

...one more person find purpose in retirement. ...one more retiree create new social connections. ...one more individual embrace a healthier and active lifestyle. ...one more reader discover a fulfilling way of life.

To get that 'feel good' feeling and help this person for real, all you have to do is...and it takes less than 60 seconds... leave a review.

Simply scan the QR code below to leave your review:

If you feel good about helping a faceless retiree, you are my kind of person. Welcome to the club. You're one of us.

I'm that much more excited to help you enjoy an exciting retirement more than you can possibly imagine. You'll love the lessons I'm about to share in the coming chapters.

Thank you from the bottom of my heart. Now, back to our regularly scheduled programming.

Your biggest fan,

Victoria Spring

PS - Fun fact: If you provide something of value to another person, it makes you more valuable to them. If you'd like goodwill straight from another retiree - and you believe this book will help them send this book their way.

RETIRE, ROAM, REDISCOVER... REPEAT!

"People don't take trips, trips take people."

— JOHN STEINBECK

WHY RETIRE, ROAM, REDISCOVER AND REPEAT?

Here are a few benefits that will entice you to retire as an opportunity to roam and rediscover more in life and stick to that routine for a long time:

- **Physical health benefits - Immunity boosting:** Travelers Worldwide states that exposure to novel surroundings and varying temperatures may bolster immunity. The body develops defenses by being exposed to various microorganisms in unfamiliar environments.
- **Reducing stress:** People may escape their routine and lower their stress levels by traveling. According to NBC News, travel may cause cortisol levels—a hormone linked to stress—to drop.

- **Mental health benefits - Increasing creativity:** Traveling exposes people to various cultures, settings, and viewpoints, which may foster creativity. According to Everyday Health, those who travel often are more likely to have inventive ideas and develop novel solutions. **• Lessening anxiety and depression:** According to GoodRx, traveling might lessen anxiety and depression symptoms. Experiencing a shift in environment and trying out new things might be beneficial for mental health. **• Increasing happiness:** According to Lee Health, planning for a vacation and the experience of traveling may make people happier. Exciting and joyful experiences come from traveling, which supports mental health in general.

- **General Health benefits - Encouraging heart health:** Traveling and seeing the world might benefit your heart. According to the Travel and Leisure article, travel may improve heart health, particularly to places where physical activities like climbing or walking are offered.

- **Strengthening relationships:** During travel, forming new relationships and spending time with loved ones may strengthen social ties and improve emotional health.

In conclusion, scientists believe travel has more advantages than merely fun.

Top Destinations in the US:

Charleston, South Carolina: Distinguished by its southern friendliness and historic beauty, Charleston provides seniors with a laid-back atmosphere, lovely gardens, and historical landmarks.

Sedona, Arizona: Known for its red rock vistas, art galleries, and health pursuits, Sedona offers a tranquil and refreshing atmosphere.

San Antonio, Texas: Commended for providing seniors with various recreational and cultural opportunities, as well as for its rich history, cultural attractions, and the well-known River Walk.

Mackinac Island, Michigan: With its ancient buildings and horsedrawn carriages, this car-free island is noted for its Victorian beauty, which offers seniors a glimpse into the past.

Top Destinations Abroad:

Italy: This country is recommended due to its fascinating history, stunning scenery, and lively culture. Seniors may spend time exploring historical monuments, art, and food.

Australia: Its main draws are the Great Barrier Reef, fauna, and the country's varied natural beauty. The nation provides elders with a healthy dose of adventure and leisure.

Ireland: Known for its charming towns and gorgeous scenery, Ireland offers seniors a serene and beautiful setting to explore.

Japan: Acknowledged for its sophisticated but approachable infrastructure, abundant cultural legacy, and exquisite gardens, Japan is a location that appeals to seniors seeking a blend of contemporary and traditional experiences.

These locations provide a range of senior-friendly activities and services, such as leisure options, cultural immersion, and beautiful scenery.

TRAVEL 101

Planning is essential before starting a trip, and considering the unique requirements of older citizens adds another level of thought. Let us tell the story of how to economize while meticulously organizing every vacation detail to create an unforgettable experience. A desire and a budget set the course for the voyage.

Set a budget and travel objectives (Ramsey Solutions, n.d.): When the first signs of wanderlust appear, take a seat and list your vacation objectives. Dream about the places that make hearts race. However, most of all, attach those aspirations to a spending plan. Ramsey Solutions says matching travel goals with a well-defined budget may ensure a wise and rewarding vacation.

Do the homework and select a location (Nomadic Matt, n.d.; Annie Anywhere, n.d.): Set objectives and prepare a budget, then explore the options. Annie Anywhere suggests looking at travel options that fit both budget and interests. Think about the area attractions, weather, and safety. Nomadic Matt continues, saying that this step is about creating an experience that suits tastes rather than merely deciding on a location.

Make an itinerary (Great Senior Living, n.d.; Practical Wanderlust, n.d.): Now that the canvas is prepared, the itinerary must be painted. Practical Wanderlust stresses the need for a thorough itinerary that includes lodging, transportation, and activities. Great Senior Living advises seniors to plan their travels as comfortably and conveniently as possible to make the most of every minute of the trip.

Make travel and lodging arrangements (Better Health, n.d.; Life Care Services, n.d.): Now that the strategy has solidified, it is time to implement it. Better Health and Life Care Services advises taking advantage of senior discounts when making travel and lodging reservations. For a more affordable experience, consider options like vacation rentals.

Pack light and wisely (we are global travelers, 2020): The time has come to stuff your bag. To We Are Global Travellers suggests bringing just the necessities to save money on additional baggage fees.

Utilize travel benefits (Capital One, n.d.): As we enter the digital age, astute travelers use technology. Capital One suggests looking into travel rewards to save money on travel and lodging. Travel credit cards with rewards may be used wisely to earn extra benefits and savings.

Remain adaptable and welcome local knowledge (Hey Mondo, n.d.): Hey Mondo embraces spontaneity and flexibility in travel. Consider adjusting vacation dates and keep an eye out for lastminute offers. Explore regional markets and restaurants when traveling for genuine, reasonably priced experiences.

Keep in mind the extra advice from Landmark Senior Living while traveling. Ensure everyone knows plans, especially loved ones, and prioritize health. Through weaving this story, we have outlined a road map for not only organizing a vacation but also designing an experience that is both affordable and emotionally satisfying. With meticulous preparation, the road ahead will be nothing short of an extraordinary adventure filled with discovery and fulfillment.

TEN CHEAPEST AND SAFEST DESTINATION FOR RETIREES

Simon (2023) compiled a list of the ten cheapest countries for retirees that is helpful to offer retirees more options toward their aspiring destination after retirement:

The ten most affordable nations to retire to are listed below:

Portugal: Portugal's index of the cost of living is 42.18. Portugal is one of the safest nations in the world overall, coming in at number six on the Global Peace Index. Its mild weather and sandy beaches may also provide a rejuvenating atmosphere for the latter years (Simon, 2023).

To retire in Portugal, you must provide evidence of health insurance when requesting residence at the local consulate. Nonetheless, many well-known US health insurance providers also offer coverage in Portugal, simplifying the transition.

Also, the nation recently changed its tax laws to make it more welcoming to foreigners. If granted Non-Habitual Residence (NHR) status, you will not be subject to income tax for the next ten years. This would include pension income and investment profits even if produced outside of Portugal.

Malaysia: The Cost-of-Living Index for Malaysia is 34.41 (Simon, 2023). Malaysia is a nation on our list attempting to be friendlier to foreigners. In reality, the Malaysia My Second Home (MM2H) program allows you to get a visa for a maximum of ten years.

With so many beaches and forests, the country is the perfect destination for those who like the outdoors. However, Malaysia offers a variety of metropolitan locations for people who choose to continue living city life far into old age. A few magazines have listed George Town as one of the best places in the world to retire.

If reading this from a major American metropolis, one could be drawn to Malaysia because of its affordable cost of living. In George Town, the average cost of a one-bedroom apartment is $278 in the city and $174 in the suburbs, according to Numbeo (Simon, 2023).

Furthermore, do not stress about getting over cultural shock. In Malaysia, English is referred to as the "unofficial first language." It is ranked 18 on the Index of World Peace, which puts it far higher on the peace scale than other Southeast Asian nations (Simon, 2023).

Spain: Spain has a 47.51 cost of living index, and its ranking on the Global Peace Index is 29. Spain is still a European nation known for its tranquility and generally cheap cost of living (Simon, 2023). It often appears on rankings of the top retirement destinations. Spain has many historical sites to visit, keeping one's mind and body active. Modernist paintings like Picasso, Dali, and the Baroque painter Diego Velazquez are particularly pleasing to art enthusiasts.

Additionally, foreign nationals who fit the following criteria can be eligible for the nation's public healthcare program:

- If recently separated from a spouse who makes Social Security contributions,
- If self-employed or employed, pay into Spain's social security system.
- If receiving a state pension.

Madrid is the most expensive city in Spain. However, you may still locate sites here that are far less expensive than those in large American cities. An apartment in the city center with one bedroom costs around $1,055 per month, according to the vacation website Escape Artist (Simon, 2023).

After ninety days, apply for a visa to retire to Spain.

Costa Rica: The cost-of-living index for Costa Rica is 43.65, and the country is 38th in the global peace index. Costa Rica is the ideal destination for anybody seeking to retire in a tropical paradise without paying the price for paradise. Popular San Jose rentals are around $610 a month on average, according to Numbeo. Additionally, dinners at nearby eateries start at around $7 (Simon, 2023).

It is difficult for outdoor enthusiasts to become bored here. Activities include hiking through the rainforest, horseback riding, fishing, surfing, and whitewater rafting. Additionally, you will not have to worry as much about being wounded, as the healthcare system in Costa Rica is outstanding and ranked among the best in Latin America.

Applying for a Pensionado visa will allow retirement in Costa Rica, with a monthly pension income of at least $2,500 (Simon, 2023).

Panama: Panama's Cost of Living Index is 48.25, and her ranking on the Global Peace Index is 61. According to International Living's Global Retirement Index, Panama came in first. The nation takes various steps to entice foreigners. For example, the government will not tax money made outside of the United States. One gains if contributing to a retirement plan established in the United States.

It also provides Pensionado and Friendly Nations visas if monthly income is $1,000 or more from Social Security, an annuity, or a pension qualify for the latter.

It is like a rewards credit card; the Pensionado Visa provides the following savings:

- 25% off meals, 30% off public transportation, and 25% off flights (Simon, 2023).

Lifestyle and preferred location will determine the cost of living, just as in any other region. You may survive on as low as $500 per month in Panama by forgoing certain essential comforts. A more typical but modest lifestyle would be roughly $2,000 monthly (Simon, 2023).

However, if you desire to live in Latin America, Panama can provide a good compromise between living expenses and reaching an active retirement. To keep the blood moving, engage in golf, zip-line, and biking activities, or retreat to places like Boquete. This city is well-known for being a center for well-being, offering many options for practicing Tai Chi, yoga, meditation, and other forms of physical exercise.

Czech Republic: The Czech Republic's Cost of Living Index is 44.33 and ranks eighth on the Global Peace Index (Simon, 2023). If Eastern Europe is calling, the Czech Republic may provide an excellent mix of price and security. In actuality, the Global Peace Index places it eighth. According to the international travel website Expat Focus (n.d.), this region has far lower real estate prices than much of Western Europe.

There is much to do, particularly regarding history; the Czech Republic is referred to as the world's castle capital. The Middle Ages saw the construction of the Prague Castle. Additionally, 20 structures recognized as UNESCO cultural and global heritage sites are located inside the nation.

After the first 90 days, you would have to apply for a visa with evidence of health insurance (Simon, 2023).

Peru: Peru's Index of Cost of Living is 30.74 and ranks 101 on the Global Peace Index. Regarding landscape, Peru offers a wide variety (Simon, 2023). The nation is home to peaceful rural communities and high, mountainous areas. The cost of living is often cheaper than in other Latin American countries. For example, an apartment in Lima's affluent Miraflores neighborhood is approximately $740 per month (Simon, 2023).

Moreover, enjoy internationally recognized food prepared with fresh ingredients from the sea to the mountains. A Rentista Visa is allowed with a minimum of $1,000. According to Zinn (2023), you can survive on a $1,800 or $2,000 monthly income (Zinn, 2023). At least six months a year must be in the nation but not permitted to work; eligibility for a permanent visa is after seven years.

Peru is a "high" peace nation according to the group that created the Global Peace Scale, despite Peru falling 15 places in the last year to rank 101 (Simon, 2023).

Slovenia: Slovenia's Cost of Living Index stands at 47.30, and her position is seven on the Global Peace Index. Slovenia is a good choice for those who want to retire and have a background in the Alps but cannot pay the high cost of France or Switzerland. Slovenia has several peaks, and visitors to Triglav National Park may work up a sweat there.

Ljubljana, in Slovenia, was listed by International Living as one of the best ten cities in the world to retire. Live and Invest Overseas, a group that helps companies relocate overseas, claims that for a couple, the cost is around $720 per month for a comfortable apartment rental in Ljubljana (Simon, 2023).

Austria: Austria's Global Peace Index Ranking is 5, with the Costof-Living Index at 64.11. Austria is among the world's top 10 most livable countries despite being somewhat more costly than the other nations on our list (Simon, 2023). A recent Economist Intelligence Unit assessment named Vienna the world's most livable city.

One city has an almost limitless selection of world-class museums, great art, and architectural masterpieces. According to Numbeo, an apartment in Vienna averages $960.

After six months, a residency visa is needed to retire here, and evidence of income is required to get one.

Australia: Australia is 72.27 on the Cost-of-Living Index, and her ranking on the Global Peace Index is 27. Australia has a higher average cost of living than most other nations on our list, although it has declined recently. In the city center, living expenditures, including rent, may range from $1,000 to $2,000 per month, according to Numbeo (Simon, 2023).

Additionally, visit one of the numerous beaches in the nation to take in the tranquility and laid-back atmosphere. Animal enthusiasts may take sightseeing trips to observe wombats, kangaroos, and other indigenous animals.

Retirement here may be more complicated than in other locations on our list. First of all, the nation did away with the Retirement Visa in 2018. However, to meet eligibility, the below-listed requirements must be fulfilled to get an Investor Retirement Visa:

- Have at least 55 years of age;
- Live and work in Australia for a maximum of four years; Make a
- minimum income dependent on location and invest a certain amount of money in the nation.

Australia provides various visas to attract individuals who can boost the nation's economy. Therefore, it can be the ideal location for seniors who want to work part-time. A family member may also sponsor a visitor. If not, apply for a visitor's visa and submit another one as needed (Simon, 2023).

Keeping Safe While Traveling

Seniors, in particular, need to ensure they are safe while traveling and not at home. The following essential safety precautions have been extracted from the offered links to assist readers in preventing avoidable mishaps, wounds, or unpleasant experiences:

Be well-informed and prepared: Smarter Travel advises seniors to do their homework and stay current on their destination. Being aware of local laws, traditions, and health hazards is helpful when making travel plans and preparing for a safe trip.

Select accommodations judiciously: Senior Travel Central strongly emphasizes booking lodgings with security features. Select well-known hotels for their security, close access to emergency exits, and well-lit entrances.

Protect vital records: Health in Aging advises photocopying critical documents, such as insurance policies and passports. Carry the copies apart and keep the originals safe.

Maintain Communication: The National Council on Aging (NCOA) emphasizes the importance of maintaining contact with loved ones when traveling. Frequent check-ins provide comfort and quick help when required.

Make medicine and health a priority: Every source emphasizes the importance of NCOA, Health in Aging, and Senior Travel Central. Keep a basic first aid kit on hand, carry a sufficient supply of prescriptions, and be informed of the medical services in the area.

Use caution while handling valuables: Smarter Travel advises seniors to use caution when handling valuables. When carrying essentials, use discrete accessories instead of flaunting bulky bills or pricey jewelry.

Exercise alertness in public areas: Senior Travel Central advises using caution while in public areas. To avoid dangers, keep an eye on the surroundings, especially in busy places.

Make use of dependable transportation: Health in Aging emphasizes how crucial it is to choose dependable modes of transportation. To guarantee safety while traveling, give priority to reliable transportation providers.

Remain hydrated and aware of physical limitations: NCOA advises elders to be mindful of their physical limitations and to drink plenty of water. To avoid fatigue, modify activities according to energy levels and take rests.

Being ready for emergencies: Smarter Travel emphasizes emergency preparation. Maintain easy access to emergency contact details and have a strategy in place for unforeseen circumstances.

In conclusion, prioritizing safety while traveling entails extensive study, thoughtful planning, and constant alertness. These safety precautions allow seniors to travel more comfortably while lowering risk.

Travel Etiquette That Makes a Big Difference

Traveling is more than simply seeing new locations; it is also about being a considerate tourist and appreciating the local way of life. To guarantee a courteous and enjoyable experience for all parties, let's explore the plethora of travel etiquette advice found at the sites supplied:

Honor regional traditions and customs: Riviera Travel and Small Business Trends stress how important it is to honor regional traditions (Riviera Travel, n.d.; Small Business Trends, 2023). To demonstrate respect for the host nation, get familiar with its customs, dress regulations, and cultural norms.

Be aware of the volume: True Travels advises paying attention to noise levels, particularly in public areas and lodgings (True Travels, n.d.). In public places, keep talks at a tolerable level and use headphones.

Arrive on time: Sim Options emphasizes the value of being on time (Sim Options, n.d.). Being punctual shows consideration for other people's schedules, whether meeting with locals or on a guided tour.

Take careful pictures: When taking photographs, Expat Explore advises being considerate of others' privacy (Expat Explore, n.d.). Please take photos of people only with their permission, particularly in places with sensitive cultural or religious contexts.

Reduce the adverse effect on the environment: The Early Airway (The Early Airway, n.d.) emphasizes the significance of reducing environmental effects. To protect the area's natural beauty, dispose of garbage properly, stick to approved pathways, and make eco-friendly decisions.

Acquire some basic local words: Both Sim Options and Riviera Travel emphasize the need to be familiar with some basic local vocabulary (Riviera Travel, n.d.; Sim Options, n.d.). Locals love it when others try to converse in their language, even if it is only a few hellos.

Wear proper clothes: According to Small Business Trends (2023), travelers should dress according to the weather at their location. Respecting cultural norms demonstrates cultural sensitivity.
Certain religious places or activities may have clothing rules.

Show respect for locals: According to The Early Airway (n.d.), it is recommended to show respect for the inhabitants. Respect their traditions, be courteous, and make an effort to engage in constructive dialogue that leaves a good impression.

Recognize tipping customs: Sim Options suggests learning about tipping customs. Tipping may not be expected in some nations, while it may be a fundamental aspect of service culture in others.

Keep an open mind: Expat Explore stresses the significance of keeping an open mind (Expat Explore, n.d.). Accept cultural and viewpoint differences to make the trip more fulfilling and richer.

Tried and Tested Travel Tips

Seniors may travel more comfortably and conveniently if they use these helpful recommendations. With information from reliable sources, the following travel tips for seniors are tried and true:

Stay hydrated in-flight: Bring a refillable water bottle to guarantee hydration during flights and ask flight attendants to fill it (Flying et al.).

Use compression socks: To enhance blood circulation and lower the possibility of leg swelling while flying, use compression socks.

Optimize packing with Ziplock bags: To keep baggage tidy and readily accessible, arrange clothing, toiletries, and other necessities in different Ziplock bags (Savoteur, n.d.).

Carry a portable charger: Keep electronics charged on extended trips or while visiting new places (Blakeford, n.d.).

Research senior discounts: Benefit from senior discounts provided by dining establishments, transportation providers, and attractions.

Use a neck pillow for comfort: To avoid neck discomfort on lengthy flights or travels, pack a neck cushion for extra comfort.

Plan rest stops on road trips: Arrange rest breaks to stretch, take a stroll, and generally improve the comfort of the travel (Savoteur, n.d.).

Make use of travel apps: To improve convenience when traveling, make use of travel applications for directions, translation, and locating nearby services.

Invest in comfortable footwear: To make lengthy walks or expeditions more pleasant, spend money on supportive and comfy shoes.

Consider travel insurance: To have extra peace of mind and be covered for unforeseen circumstances, consider purchasing travel insurance.

Using these helpful travel tips, seniors may have a much easier and more pleasurable time traveling. Every suggestion is meant to improve ease and comfort on the trip, from packing efficiently to keeping hydrated.

Essential Packing Checklist

Make sure the trip is stress-free and pleasurable by utilizing our extensive packing list designed for seniors. Knowledge from reliable sources and the following advice can help to pack effectively:

Clothes:

Cozy Ensembles: Wear airy, loose attire to provide comfort while traveling, suitable for the destination's weather.

Footwear: Supportive, cozy shoes that are appropriate for strolling. Easy slip-on shoes or slippers for use in hotels **Accessories:** A cap or hat to shield against the sun. Sunglasses for eye protection.

Personal belongings:

Medications: Sufficient supply of over-the-counter and prescription drugs. Prescription contact lenses and/or spectacles.

Health Essentials: Include a first aid pack with necessary medical items, sanitizing wipes, and hand sanitizer.

Toiletries: Toiletries in travel-sized containers, such as toothpaste, shampoo, and toothbrush. Items for personal hygiene.

Travel Documents:

Identification and Important Documents: The document includes a driver's license, passport, and other necessary identification. Contact information and data on travel insurance are also included.

Travel Itinerary: A copy of the itinerary, either printed or digital, with hotel reservations and contact information.

Entertainment and Technology:

Electronic Devices: Tablet, smartphone, or e-reader. Device chargers for electronics.

Entertainment: For leisure, novels, e-books, or audiobooks. Headphones for private listening.

Comfort and Safety:

Travel Blanket and Pillow: A neck cushion to make travel more comfortable. A thin blanket for extra warmth.

Safety Items for Travel: A neck bag or money belt to keep valuables safe. Emergency flashlight.

Miscellaneous:

Snacks: Nutritious snacks and a reusable water container.

Adapters and Chargers: Power adapters for outlets unique to a specific location. A portable electronic gadget charger.

Extras for Specific Trips:

Outdoor activities: Use bug repellent and sunscreen for outdoor activities, and carry an umbrella or rain cover.

Cruise Specific: Dress code for dining on cruise ships. If necessary, move illness treatments.

Beginning with our interactive packing checklist ensures a smooth trip. Tailor it according to your travel style, destination, and personal preferences. While packing, mark off items to ensure everything is remembered. Happy travels!

Welcome to "Retiring Strong," the sixth chapter. As we progress, we reach a critical stage centered on resiliency, self-determination, and accepting our inner strength. Prepare to achieve your greatest potential and approach retirement with enthusiasm and confidence. As we map our path to a purposeful and happy retirement, it is time to embrace the power of resilience.

"The groundwork of all happiness is health."

— *LEIGH HUNT*

DIET AND EXERCISE: FUELING YOUR BODY FOR AN ENERGETIC RETIREMENT

T he golden years, ahh, are the best times in life to cherish. How better to celebrate these years than to put health first with a nutritious diet and vigorous exercise? Let's discuss nutrition and why it is so essential for aging gracefully and learn clever tricks for a delicious and healthy meal.

Tuning into nutritional needs: Adjusting your diet to suit the body's evolving requirements is critical to starting this new phase of life. According to Healthline, a healthy diet customized to meet the specific nutritional needs of elderly citizens should be prioritized.

Nutritional Ensemble

Let's examine the leading musicians in the nutritional symphony, each responsible for helping you age gracefully.

Protein powerhouse: The primary ingredient is protein, which is essential for both maintaining and repairing muscles. To guarantee enough protein in your diet, include lean meats, beans, and dairy products (Better Health, n.d.).

Calcium cadence: Calcium is the most essential mineral for maintaining bone health. To provide robust skeletal support, include dairy, fortified plant-based milk, and leafy greens in meals (NIDirect, n.d.).

Hydration harmony: As you age, staying hydrated becomes essential to maintaining maximum health. Keep your body well hydrated with the elixir of life, water, herbal beverages, and hydrating fruits (NCOA, n.d.).

Fiber flourish: Fiber takes center stage, supporting gut health and helping with weight control. To promote general well-being, make whole grains, fruits, and vegetables nutritional pillars (HelpGuide, n.d.).

Recipe Knowledge for Snacking: A Delectable Summary

Palette of vibrancy: Apply a rainbow of colors on your plate, each signifying a distinct vitamin. This not only makes food look better but also guarantees a nutrient-dense eating experience.

Portion poise: Learn to regulate portion sizes and take time to enjoy every mouthful. This promotes overall well-being by assisting with weight control and aiding in digestion.

Savvy substitutions: Make wise substitutions; choose whole grains over processed ones, and use aromatic herbs and spices to season food rather than adding too much salt.

Social suppers: Make mealtimes become special get-togethers with those you care about. Over healthful meals, have fun discussions that promote mental and physical well-being via moments of connection.

The nutritional symphony is now in motion, so let us move on to the workout dance. According to the Cleveland Clinic (n.d.) and Canada's Food Guide (n.d.), frequent physical exercise is the key to gracefully aging.

THE EXERCISE BALLET: STEPS TO VITALITY

Embark on a dance with the following steps:

- **Aerobic Flourish:** Take part in aerobic workouts such as swimming, cycling, or walking. They keep your heart content and vitality high.
- **Strength Staccato:** The main focus is strength training, which increases metabolism while maintaining muscular mass. Accept sports like resistance training or weightlifting.
- **Flexibility Waltz:** The waltz's flexibility keeps joints agile. Tai chi or yoga are excellent dancing partners for increasing flexibility.
- **Balance Ballet:** Lastly, the ballet of balance prevents falls. Stability may be improved with basic workouts like one-

foot standing or adding balancing difficulties to your program.

Remember that enjoying the pleasure of making thoughtful decisions is more important than adhering to a strict schedule as you set out on the path toward health and vitality. So, let us celebrate the incredible partnership of an active and energetic retirement: the dietary symphony and the dance of exercise!

The key to eternal youth is not found in a legendary spring but in the cadence of physical activity designed for the elegant aging dance. Together, we will explore several fitness activities that improve energy levels, create an easy-to-follow regimen, and even provide a fun sample to get the fitness party started.

Embrace with Enthusiasm Experts must strike a balance between challenging exercises and mild warnings while navigating the fitness landscape. As per Senior Lifestyle, the following is a brief guide:

- **Walking Wonders:** A timeless classic for tailoring speed, and walking is easy on the joints.
- **Aquatic Bliss:** Swimming and water aerobics provide full body exercise with little impact.
- **Balancing Act:** Balance-enhancing exercises, such as yoga or tai chi, increase stability and reduce the risk of falls.
- *Tiptoe with Caution*
- **High-Impact Avoidance:** To protect joints, reduce high impact exercises like jogging.
- **Jerky Motion Discouragement:** Motions that are jerky or have sudden direction shifts might be dangerous.

RETIRING STRONG |

Creating Your Own Fitness Regimen - A Practical Workout Plan
Now that the scene is established, let us design a simple yet effective workout regimen. Using ideas from Arbor Company and Verywell Fit, the following regimen is created to be fun and consistent:

Waltz to Warm Up (5 minutes): To wake up your muscles, gently rotate your arms and legs.

15-minute Cardio Calypso: Take pleasure in a little stroll, whether it is on a treadmill or outside.

10-minute Strength Serenade: Bodyweight workouts such as leg lifts while sitting, wall push-ups, and squats.

Ten-minute Flexibility Fiesta: Exercises like sitting forward bends and shoulder stretches that improve flexibility.

Ballet in Balance (5 minutes): Include balance exercises such as heel-to-toe walking and standing on one leg at a time.

5-minute Cool-Down Crescendo: Calm stretches that target the main muscle groups to help cool down.

Embarking on Your Fitness Adventure: A Supportive Guide

After retirement, maintaining fitness does not have to be complicated. The National Institute on Aging (NIA) suggests the following helpful advice to make your exercise journey enjoyable:

Start Slowly: Start with enjoyable activities and progressively boost the level of difficulty.

Listen to Your Body: Observe how your body reacts and modify the regimen as necessary.

Make It Social: If you need more incentive, take a fitness class or participate in activities with friends.

Mix It Up: Incorporate activities into your schedule to keep things fresh.

After retirement, becoming healthy is about enjoying movement, pleasure, and a renewed feeling of well-being. Allow the music to continue while moving to the beat of the workout, leading to vigor, strength, and a joyful dance during your later years.

Advice for Staying Engaged: Savor the Liveliness of Retirement

Greetings from the journey of maintaining an active lifestyle into old age, where each stride is an expression of health and energy! Together, we will unearth a wealth of knowledge, understanding, and joyful techniques to keep the body and soul vibrating with vitality as you embark on an adventure.

Dancing through everyday situations: Retirement is a vast ballroom, where each step is a dance move. Allow the beat of life to guide you, whether that means dancing to your favorite music while performing tasks around the home or taking spontaneous dance breaks (Explore Retirement Living).

Exercise and socialize hand in hand: Social relationships have unparalleled power. Engage in social activities to keep active and enjoy the delight of companionship. The advantages of remaining active are enhanced by the social experiences of participating in sports leagues, walking clubs, and fitness programs (Samuel C. Shockaday & Associates).

Unleash your hobbies' potential: Retirement is the ideal time to explore hobbies. Hobbies like cycling, golfing, and gardening keep you active and provide a daily routine with a sense of excitement and purpose. Interests might serve as the foundation for an exciting and dynamic existence.

Accept the magnificent outdoors: Retirement provides the time to answer nature's call. Explore hiking paths and strolls, or enjoy the beauty of parks. The great outdoors serves as a playground, encouraging you to keep moving and take in all the world offers (Health News, n.d.).

Make exercise a daily routine: Like a thread in a tapestry, include movement in each day of retirement life. A few quick stretches, yoga poses, or other easy activities in the morning will help you feel good all day. Maintaining consistency in these regular routines fosters an active lifestyle.

Combine exercise with recreation: Leisure is a moment for active relaxation, not slouching around. Select recreational pursuits that require physical activity, like swimming, kayaking, or even a relaxed round of golf. In this manner, you keep busy and have fun during leisure (Explore Retirement Living).

Make achievable fitness objectives: Strive for attainable fitness objectives. Setting and reaching objectives increases motivation and a feeling of success, whether raising the number of steps each day, learning a new yoga posture, or progressively increasing the intensity of your exercise regimen.

Combine and contrast activities: Vary routines to keep things interesting. Alternate between strength training, walking, cycling, and swimming. Being active is a fascinating and fun experience that targets various muscle groups and avoids boredom.

Make joint-friendly exercises a priority: As the body ages, make joint-friendly exercises a priority. Choose low-impact sports like yoga, cycling, or swimming to enjoy the advantages of regular exercise while preserving your joints.

Attend to the symphony of your body: Above all, listen to your body's music. Observe its rhythms and indications. Make a specific activity an anthem if it brings happiness and seems promising. Be kind to yourself and look for other options if anything is uncomfortable. Remaining active in retirement is an opportunity to savor the vibrant aspects of life, not a duty. Every hint is a brushstroke, depicting a lively, happy, and contented retirement.

Matters of the Heart: Taking Care of Your Heart During the Golden Years

Welcome to the symphony of aging, where a happy, full life is synchronized to the beating of a healthy heart. Let's explore the positive relationship between retirement, aging, and heart health and share some doable strategies to keep the heart humming with energy.

The Heart's Encore: Heart Health and Aging: The aging process and the development of heart health are normal. The National Institute on Aging (NIA) states that it is critical to comprehend how our cardiovascular system ages. The heart's efficiency may gradually deteriorate, blood vessels constrict, and arteries harden. However, information and proactive decision-making strengthen the path to heart-healthy aging.

Embracing the Serenade of Your Heart - Useful Advice for Seniors

Let's take a delightful tour, delving into practical advice that captures the spirit of heart health for seniors:

Healthy Eating - A Fond Celebration: Adopt a heart-healthy diet full of fiber, antioxidants, and omega-3 fatty acids. To make the platter colorful, add fatty fish, avocados, almonds, berries, and leafy greens (Grandoaks DC n.d.).

Stay Active - The Heart's Pas de Deux: Exercise regularly to suit comfort and degree of fitness. Try to engage in heart-rate-raising activities like dancing, swimming, or brisk walking. Senior Services of America said, "It's a joyful way to keep the heart in its rhythmic dance."

Heart-Healthy Living Options: Manage stress, abstain from tobacco, and limit alcohol consumption to improve heart health. A healthy heart echoes the music of well-being formed by these lifestyle choices.

Frequent Heart Exams - A Harmonious Preventive Measure: Arrange routine examinations to track cholesterol, blood pressure, and general heart health. Your heart will continue to pump vigorously if early identification enables prompt interventions.

Social Links - Emotional Ties: Foster happy and emotionally healthy social relationships. A rich tapestry of family relationships and friendships enriches a heart that beats with pleasure.

Heart-Healthy Checklist - Making Wellness Easier: Simplify the process by using a checklist that promotes heart health. A quick checklist will help ensure you always care for your heart health, from food to exercise.

A Fond Farewell: Your Harmony of Health

Remember, during this uplifting symphony's grand conclusion, retirement, and age are not obstacles but doors leading to a heart healthy encore.

Medical Insurance in Brief: An All-Inclusive Guide for Seniors

Starting the golden years of retirement is an exciting trip and a time when careful preparation becomes critical, particularly concerning health. Having health insurance is essential to having a safe and fulfilling retirement. Now, let us explore the what, why, and what factors to consider while negotiating the world of retiree health insurance.

Why Invest in Insurance? Exposition of the Safety Net

- **Safety in Uncertain Times:** Although retirement offers the gift of leisure and relaxation, it also comes with unknowns. Medical insurance acts as a strong safety net in the event of unforeseen medical difficulties, offering financial security (Insular Life, n.d.).
- **Maintaining Financial Health:** The price of medical treatment may add up quickly. By paying for medical costs, insurance protects financial stability and lets you enjoy retirement without worrying about crippling debt (Stanley, n.d.).
- **Peace of mind and legacy planning:** Insurance has become a tool for personal well-being and legacy planning. It provides financial stability and peace of mind by safeguarding loved ones.
- **Things to Prioritize Around the Insurance Market Entire**
- **Coverage:** When selecting an insurance plan, prioritize comprehensive coverage. Seek insurance that covers a variety of medical requirements, such as regular checkups and serious diseases (FWD Philippines). **Flexibility and Affordability:** Evaluate the insurance plans' flexibility and affordability. Select solutions that will fit the budget and allow for adjusting changing health demands as you age (Auto Home Boat Insurance). **Designed to Meet Your Needs:** Every retiree has different healthcare requirements. To ensure you do not pay for unneeded coverage and get enough help when it counts, consider insurance that can be customized to your unique health needs (U.S. News & World Report). **Transparency and Reputation:** Look for insurance companies with a track record of honesty and dependability. Choose an insurance company with a reputation for having clear policies and top-notch customer service by reading reviews and evaluating client comments (Texas Department of Insurance).

Medical insurance is a protagonist that provides safety, financial stability, and peace of mind in the big story of retirement. Let medical insurance be the vital thread that keeps health and wellbeing front and center while writing the chapters of your retirement tale. This will help to savor every second of this joyous time.

Medicare: An Overview as a Guide to Health Insurance in Retirement

Retirement is a journey, and navigating the intricacies of healthcare alone is unnecessary. Medicare serves as a thorough guide and is the cornerstone of healthcare coverage for seniors. Let's dispel the myths surrounding Medicare and better grasp its fundamentals, vocabulary, available coverage, and the essential parts of this health safety net.

Medicare: What is it? Interpreting the Core: Medicare is a publicly sponsored health insurance program aimed largely at those 65 and above. Additionally, it embraces some younger people with impairments. The Medicare Payment Advisory Commission (MedPAC) states that the program is evidence of a commitment to provide access to high-quality healthcare throughout the prime retirement years.

Terms to Know: Navigating the Medicare Lexicon
Get acquainted with the following phrases before starting your Medicare journey:

- **Premium:** This is the monthly cost of having Medicare coverage, which guarantees access to necessary medical care.
- **Deductible:** You must satisfy a certain upfront payment amount before Medicare begins paying for medical costs. **Copayment**
- **and Coinsurance:** The words "copayment" and "coinsurance" describe how Medicare splits medical treatment costs.

Medicare's Essential Coverage Options

Medicare provides a range of coverage choices, each with a specific function:

Hospital insurance, or Part A, covers inpatient hospital stays as well as skilled nursing facility, home health, and hospice care.

Essential services include doctor visits, outpatient care, preventative care, and certain home health care services, which are covered under Part B (Medical Insurance).

Medicare Advantage, or Part C, is a complete option that incorporates Part A, Part B, and often Part D (prescription drugs) into a single plan. It is provided by private insurance firms.

Part D (Prescription Drug Coverage) makes access to Medicare approved private prescription drug plans possible.

Getting Around Medicare Parts - A Complete Guide

It is critical to comprehend Medicare's many components to make well-informed selections about healthcare needs:

- **CenterWell Primary Care:** Provides thorough instructions on Medicare qualifying requirements and enrollment.
- **Medicare Interactive:** Offers in-depth details on Original Medicare Parts A and B.
- **HealthPartners:** Provides comprehensive delineations of the different Medicare components to facilitate informed decision-making.

Imagine Medicare as a compass that will lead you through the confusing world of retirement healthcare once you enter its domain. Now that you are well-informed on its components, available coverage, and critical terminology, you can make wise choices and ensure your health stays your priority as you enter retirement.

The Nutritional Encore: Aging and Dietary Needs

Your body responds differently to the beginning of this new chapter, and your diet should, too. Seniors should prioritize eating a nutritious diet, according to Healthline. The requirements for nutrients change with time, with an increasing emphasis on specific vitamins and minerals.

Astute Cooking Advice: A Satisfying Recap

After establishing the nutritional framework, let's use our culinary magic to make eating healthily enjoyable.

Vibrant Color Scheme: Use a variety of colors while painting your plate. Different colors represent different nutrients, making for a visually pleasing and nutrient-dense meal.

Portion Panache: Adopt portion control and take time to appreciate every mouthful. This will facilitate proper weight management and help with digestion.

Smart Swaps: Make wise substitutions. Select whole grains over processed ones, and use herbs and spices instead of extra salt.

Social Suppers: Make dinners for gatherings with others. Have enjoyable discussions with those you care about over a healthy meal, which will improve your mental and physical health.

Workout Extravaganza: Steps to Vitality

Your nutritional symphony is now in motion, so let's move on to the workout dance. According to the Cleveland Clinic and Canada's Food Guide, frequent physical exercise is the key to gracefully aging.

Tips on How to Stay Active: Embrace the Vibrancy of Retirement
Discover the secrets to staying lively and vibrant as you embrace retirement with open arms! Let's dive into a world of tips and tricks that will keep your body and soul buzzing with energy and vitality throughout this exciting chapter of your life:

- **Embrace the rhythm of life:** Retirement is your chance to dance through each day like it's a grand ballroom. Let the music of life guide your steps, whether you're grooving to your favorite tunes while doing chores or enjoying impromptu dance breaks.
- **Stay active and socialize:** Forge meaningful connections and stay active by engaging in social activities. Join sports leagues, walking clubs, or fitness programs to keep your body moving and enjoy the camaraderie of like-minded individuals.
- **Pursue your passion:** Dive headfirst into your hobbies during retirement. Whether cycling, golfing, or gardening, let your interests light up your days and infuse your routine with excitement and purpose.
- **Embrace the great outdoors:** Answer the call of nature and explore the beauty of parks, hiking trails, and scenic strolls. Let the outdoors be your playground, encouraging you to stay active and soak in the wonders of the world. • **Incorporate daily movement:** Make exercise a seamless part of your daily routine, like weaving a thread through a tapestry. Start your mornings with gentle stretches or yoga poses to set the tone for an active and invigorating day. • **Combine exercise with leisure:** Choose recreational activities that blend relaxation with physical activity, such as swimming, kayaking, or leisurely rounds of golf. Stay engaged and have fun while keeping your body in motion during leisure time.
- **Set achievable fitness goals:** Challenge yourself with realistic fitness goals that keep you motivated and feeling accomplished. Whether increasing your daily steps, mastering a new yoga pose, or gradually intensifying your workouts, strive for success and celebrate your progress. • **Mix up your routine:** Keep things exciting by diversifying your workouts. Switch

between strength training, walking, cycling, and swimming to target different muscle groups and ward off monotony.

- **Prioritize joint-friendly exercises:** As you age, prioritize gentle exercises on your joints. Opt for low-impact activities like yoga, cycling, or swimming to reap the benefits of regular exercise while taking care of your body. **Listen to your body:** Tune in to your body's cues and rhythms. Choose activities that bring you joy and comfort and be kind to yourself by exploring alternative options if something doesn't feel right.

Retirement isn't just about slowing down; it's about embracing life's vibrancy and staying active in ways that bring you joy and fulfillment. Each tip is a stroke on the canvas of your retirement, painting a picture of vitality, happiness, and contentment.

Nurturing Your Heart's Serenade - Practical Tips for Seniors
Embark on a delightful journey through practical tips that infuse heart health with a fresh burst of vitality for seniors:

Nourish your heart with a feast of wellness: Craft a heart healthy diet bursting with fiber, antioxidants, and omega-3 fatty acids. Dive into a colorful array of foods like fatty fish, avocados, almonds, berries, and leafy greens to create a flavorful and nutritious platter. (Grandoaks DC).

Move to your heart's beat – the rhythm of fitness: Keep your heart in sync with regular exercise tailored to your comfort and fitness level. Dance, swim, or briskly walk your way to a healthy heart, embracing joyful activities that elevate your heart rate and invigorate your body. (Senior Services of America)

Harmonize your lifestyle - a focus on well-being: Cultivate heart-healthy habits by managing stress, avoiding tobacco, and moderating alcohol consumption. Let your heart sing with the melodious tune of well-being crafted by these lifestyle choices.
(Conway Medical Center)

Checkup, tune-up - prevention as the key: Stay ahead of heart health issues with routine checkups to monitor cholesterol, blood pressure, and overall cardiac wellness. Early detection paves the way for timely interventions, ensuring your heart continues to beat with vitality. (Assisting Hands)

Connect with heartfelt bonds - embracing social harmony: Cultivate meaningful and joyful social connections to enrich your heart's journey. A heart brimming with happiness thrives on the harmonious tapestry of family ties and friendships. (CHIP Reverse Mortgage)

Heart-healthy checklist - streamlining wellness: Simplify your heart health journey with a handy checklist designed to promote well-being. From nutritious eating to invigorating exercise, a quick checklist ensures you constantly nurture your heart's vitality with ease. (My Relatives Care)

A Fond Farewell: Your Harmony of Health

Remember, during this uplifting symphony's grand conclusion, retirement, and age aren't obstacles but doors leading to a hearthealthy encore. Implementing these suggestions into your routine, you are taking care of your heart and creating a lovely health symphony that will ensure your heart beats at the proper tempo for the joyful ride ahead.

Plans for Well-being: Unveiling the Options and Choosing Wisely

It might be confusing to navigate the complex maze of well-being plans, but don't worry—this book will help you go through the possibilities and choose the plan that best suits your requirements for medical care.

Various Plans: A Thorough Overview

Making selections regarding your healthcare coverage requires knowledge of the various Medicare programs. Let us examine the merits and demerits of some necessary plans:

It might be overwhelming to enter the world of Medicare plans, but don't worry—this guide will help you choose the right plan for your requirements by illuminating the way ahead.

Exploring the Landscape: An In-Depth Examination

You must be aware of the wide range of Medicare programs to make wise choices about your medical coverage. Let's examine the benefits and factors to take into account in essential plans:

Medicare Original Parts A and B

Advantages: Complete hospital and medical service coverage and the flexibility to choose any healthcare provider in the country that accepts Medicare.

Cons: Medicare Part D covers prescription drugs but at an additional cost. Deductibles and copayments can add up over time. **Medicare Part C**

Benefit

Advantages: Bundled insurance often includes Parts A, B, and D, as well as possible extra benefits like dental and eye care.

Cons: There are few healthcare provider network alternatives, and there may be yearly plan modifications.

Medicare Supplement Insurance, or Medigap

Positives: Provides predictable out-of-pocket costs and bridges Original Medicare's coverage gaps.

Cons: Does not include prescription medication coverage and requires premium payments in addition to Original Medicare.

You may confidently navigate the Medicare maze by thoroughly understanding these plan specifics and ensuring your selected coverage will completely suit your healthcare objectives and preferences.

Choosing the Right Plan: Considerations for a Tailored Approach

When choosing the best Medicare plan for your particular circumstances, there are a few critical factors to take into account:

Evaluating your medical care needs: Start by assessing your present state of health and planning for any future medical needs. This is the cornerstone for determining how much coverage is needed for this evaluation.

Evaluating costs and budget: Make sure monthly premiums, deductibles, and out-of-pocket costs fit within your means. Being aware of these expenses upfront may prevent future financial hardship.

Examining prescription medication coverage: If you depend on prescriptions, prioritize plans that provide complete pharmaceutical coverage. This guarantees that you won't have to pay a disproportionate amount of money out of pocket to get the drugs you need.

Verifying network providers: Find out whether the plan's network includes your preferred healthcare providers. Your level of satisfaction with the plan may vary greatly depending on your ability to see physicians and experts with whom you are acquainted.

Exploring additional benefits: Consider plans that include additional benefits, such as dental, vision, and wellness programs. Beyond offering essential medical treatment, these advantages may improve your healthcare experience.

By carefully weighing these criteria, you may choose a Medicare plan that meets your present medical requirements and gives you peace of mind for the future.

See NCOA's 7-Point Checklist for a comprehensive Medicare Advantage plan guide.

Remember that information is your most valuable asset when choosing a Medicare plan. If you comprehend each plan's subtleties and consider your healthcare requirements, you can navigate the Medicare landscape with clarity and confidence.

Selecting Your Medicare Plan: A Comprehensive Guide to the Best Medical Coverage

Choosing a Medicare plan may be daunting, but don't worry—this comprehensive guide will help you sort through the complexities and arrive at an option that will work well for your healthcare requirements.

Step 1: Assess Your Healthcare Needs: Start by assessing your present state of health and estimating your future requirements. Consider elements like prescribed drugs, favored medical providers, and any particular medical issues.

Step 2: Understand Plan Options: Learn about the many Medicare plans offered. Examine the benefits and drawbacks of Medicare Supplement Insurance (Medigap), Medicare Advantage (Part C), and Original Medicare (Parts A and B). Understanding the subtleties of each plan is essential as they cater to distinct demands (Investopedia).

Step 3: Compare Plans: Make use of Internet resources and tools to evaluate various Medicare plans. Interactive tools are available on websites like Humana and Health Partners to make the process of comparing easier.

Step 4: Examine Expenses: Examine the costs associated with each plan, such as the premiums, deductibles, and out-of-pocket expenses. Make sure the plan offers complete coverage while staying within your means.

Step 5: Verify Coverage for Prescription Drugs: If you need prescription drugs, get a plan with comprehensive drug coverage. Check the formulary (TDI Texas) to ensure your meds are covered.

Enrollment Periods: Choosing the Correct Time: It's essential to comprehend Medicare enrollment times. Understanding these deadlines guarantees easy access to healthcare, regardless of the Initial Enrollment Period, General Enrollment Period, or Special Enrollment Period. Aetna Medicare and Humana have further information regarding these times.

Optimizing Your Gains - optimization suggestions: Once registered, use these practical tips to get the most out of your Medicare benefits:

- The Motley Fool offers advice on how to maximize Medicare benefits.
- Kiplinger provides seven-pointers for optimizing advantages. UnitedHealthcare provides helpful advice on maximizing your
- Medicare spending.

Options for Health Insurance Before Medicare Eligibility: Filling the Gap

Solving the healthcare coverage gap for those who retire before turning 65 is imperative. The Journal of Accountancy, Kiplinger, and Merrill Lynch can help you investigate your alternatives and close the insurance gap.

Extra resources from GoodRx, Verywell Health, and Money Geek provide in-depth analyses of health insurance choices for early retirees.

Navigating the Medicare landscape takes experience, but with these tools and techniques, you can proceed with confidence and get the best possible healthcare coverage for your requirements.

Senior Living at Its Healthiest: Proven Advice

Aging doesn't mean you have to lose energy; on the contrary, it's an opportunity to prioritize your health and well-being. Here, we've compiled expert guidance from dependable sources to help you realize your vision of being the strongest and healthiest version of yourself.

Continue Your Exercise: A healthy lifestyle starts with exercise. Incorporate activities suitable for your current fitness level, such as walking, swimming, or gentle yoga. Aim for at least 150 minutes of moderate intensity exercise every week to maintain flexibility and enhance cardiovascular health (Banner Health).

Give Priority to Nutrient-Rich Foods: A well-balanced diet is necessary for overall health. Nutrient-dense foods include whole grains, fruits, vegetables, lean meats, dairy products, and dairy alternatives. Pay particular attention to these items. An adequate diet enhances immune system performance, bone health, and energy levels (NIDDK).

Regular Medical Exams: Routine examinations are crucial for detecting issues early on. Make an appointment with your physician regularly to monitor vital signs such as blood pressure, cholesterol, and other conditions. Be proactive in managing your health to maintain a high level of life (Everyday Health).

Acknowledge mental health: Maintaining cognitive health is essential. Engage in cognitively demanding pursuits such as reading, solving puzzles, and learning new abilities. Prioritize your mental health and promote social engagement to combat loneliness (FamilyDoctor, n.d.).

Sufficient Hydration: Although sometimes overlooked, maintaining enough hydration is crucial for overall health. Throughout the day, drink enough water to support healthy skin, digestion, and bodily functions.

Restful Sleep: A healthy lifestyle depends on getting enough sleep. Ensure you have a consistent sleep routine, a comfortable resting environment, and 7-9 hours of sleep per night.

Reduce stress: Make use of techniques to reduce stress, such as mindfulness, deep breathing, or engaging in fun hobbies. The capacity to manage ongoing stress is essential since it may negatively impact your physical and mental health.

Regular checkups for the eyes and teeth: Remember how important it is to keep your eyes and teeth healthy. Make periodic checkups a priority to maintain excellent oral and visual hygiene and ensure that any issues are promptly treated.

Limit your alcohol and tobacco use: Moderation is essential when it comes to alcohol use, and quitting smoking is very beneficial. Reduce or stop these practices immediately since they may be harmful to your health.

Preserve Social Connections: Mental wellness depends on maintaining social bonds. To live a happy and healthy life, maintain social relationships with friends, family, and community groups.

By adopting these techniques into a daily routine, you may notice a significant improvement in your overall well-being. Remember that living a healthy lifestyle may contribute to an enjoyable and fulfilling senior year. Age, after all, is only a number.

Let's go to Mental Wealth: Developing a Sound Mind for a Joyful Retirement," Chapter 7. This chapter explores strategies for cultivating inner serenity, resiliency, and optimism, as well as the invaluable resource of mental health. As we prioritize mental wellbeing in our pursuit of happiness and fulfillment, be ready to expand your mind and enhance your retirement experience.

MENTAL WEALTH: NURTURING A HEALTHY MIND FOR A HAPPY RETIREMENT

"As you grow older, you will discover that you have two hands, one for helping yourself, the other for helping others."

— *SAM LEVENSON*

UNDERSTANDING THE AGING BRAIN

The aging process begins with gradual changes in our bodies, starting with the brain, our most complex organ. In this section, we will examine the effects of aging on our brains and how this affects our thinking.

Structural changes: Due to structural changes, the volume and weight of the aging brain diminish. The prefrontal cortex and hippocampus are two areas of the brain that may diminish with age, according to research from the National Institute on Aging (NIA, n.d.).

Changes in hormones and neurotransmitters: Hormones, neurotransmitters, and chemical messengers in our brains all change with time. This may affect how brain cells communicate with one another and affect mood, memory, and cognitive performance (Medical News Today, n.d.).

Cognitive changes: Cognitive alterations brought on by aging may impact multitasking, memory, and processing speed. The Mailman School of Public Health at Columbia University claims that these alterations are a normal process and that knowledge of them enables people to modify their ways of thinking (Columbia University, n.d.).

Neurotransmitter function: Dopamine and serotonin are two examples of neurotransmitters that are essential to brain function. Changes in these levels may occur with aging, affecting mood, motivation, and general cognitive function (BrainFacts, 2019).

Adaptability and wisdom: The aging brain is very adaptive despite these changes. New findings demonstrate how the brain can restructure itself and create new connections, adding knowledge and skill (Medical News Today, n.d.).

Lifestyle influences: Diet, exercise, and mental stimulation are examples of lifestyle variables that may significantly influence brain health. Mentally taxing tasks like solving puzzles or learning a new skill may enhance cognitive resilience (NCBI, 2008).

People who are aware of the complexities of the aging brain are better able to make decisions that promote cognitive health. A comprehensive strategy that considers one's physical and emotional health may help one have a happy and rewarding journey through old age.

How to Use It, so You Don't Lose It - Strategies to Keep Your Brain Sharp

As we age, consistent exercise helps our brains just as much as it does our bodies. Maintaining cognitive health starts with identifying the warning signals that your brain may require additional care.

Signs you need to exercise your brain more: Early treatments for moderate cognitive impairment depend on recognizing its symptoms. These may include difficulties focusing, memory loss, and difficulty making decisions (Mayo Clinic, n.d.). If you see any of these symptoms, it is critical to speak with a healthcare provider so they can properly assess you and provide advice.

Activities to Keep Your Mind Sharp and Slow Down Brain Aging

Participating in activities that strengthen the brain may enhance cognitive vitality. Let's examine mental workouts, pursuits, routines, and advice for maintaining mental acuity and delaying the aging process.

Brain-Boosting Exercises and Activities

Mental CrossFit: Test and improve your cognitive stamina by engaging in mentally taxing activities like crosswords, Sudoku, and puzzles (Healthline, n.d.). Examine brain-training applications intended to enhance cognitive functioning and maintain mental acuity.

Creative pursuits: To exercise your brain and promote creativity, try artistic pursuits like painting, drawing, or playing an instrument.

General Habits and Tips for Cognitive Health

Balanced nutrition: Prioritize a diet with vitamins, omega-3 fatty acids, and antioxidants. These nutrients promote cognitive function by lowering inflammation and improving joint health.

Exercise: Include regular physical exercise in your routine for improved blood flow to the brain for brain health and cognitive function.

Social networks: Because social engagement is essential for cognitive health, maintaining strong social ties is crucial for mental clarity and emotional well-being.

Quality sleep: Prioritize getting enough restorative sleep to enhance memory consolidation and general cognitive performance.

By including these routines and activities, you may cultivate a brain-friendly lifestyle that enhances cognitive function and general well-being. Mental exercise is essential to keeping a bright and flexible mind, just as physical exercise benefits a healthy body.

Exploring the Impact of Nutritious Foods on Mental Well-being

Foods that support mental health: It's essential to include some nutrients in your diet that are proven to improve mental performance if you want to maximize cognitive function:

Fatty fish: Add fatty fish, such as salmon, sardines, and trout, to your diet for vital omega-3 fatty acids that can promote brain function and help prevent cognitive loss due to aging (BBC Good Food, n.d.).

Blueberries: Blueberries are high in antioxidants and have neuroprotective properties that improve memory and cognitive performance (Healthline, n.d.).

Broccoli: Including broccoli in your diet may help prevent cognitive decline and maintain normal brain function by providing antioxidants and vitamin K (Harvard Health Publishing, n.d.).

Eat these mood-boosting foods: Moods and mental health can be affected by foods consumed:

Dark chocolate: Flavonoid-rich dark chocolate can increase cerebral blood flow, which may enhance mood and cognitive performance (CNBC, 2022).

Fermented foods: Rich in bacteria, fermented foods like kefir and yogurt may have a favorable impact on gut health, which can enhance mood and mental clarity.

Nuts and seeds: Rich in minerals, including omega-3 fatty acids and magnesium, nuts, and seeds have been linked to improved mood management and cognitive function (Real Simple, n.d.).

You may enhance your mental health and foster optimum cognitive function by including these mood-enhancing and brain boosting items in your diet.

Including these mood- and brain-boosting foods in your diet is a delicious method of promoting emotional and cognitive wellbeing. A well-fed brain is robust and prepared to take on the demands of the day.

Nourishing Your Soul: A Guide to Mental Well-being After Retirement

Retirement is a significant change in life that should be carefully considered in terms of mental health. Learning about prevalent problems and looking for opportunities to give back to the community may significantly enhance a happy and psychologically sound retirement.

Navigating Mental Health Challenges in Retirement

Adapting to change: As retirement draws near, starting a new chapter in life may be fraught with uncertainty and grief. Adjusting while switching to a new routine and way of life is necessary, and some upheaval is expected during this time (HelpGuide, n.d.).

Concerns about money: Retirement's financial ramifications often loom big, producing worry and anxiety. After retirement, managing one's money becomes crucial to reducing financial stress and preserving mental health (NerdWallet, n.d.).

Loneliness and isolation: Retirement may sometimes lead to social isolation, a silent nemesis that undermines mental wellbeing. Fostering social ties is important since loneliness may worsen in the absence of regular encounters and professional camaraderie (Aviva, n.d.).

Retirement Volunteering - Finding Contentment by Giving Back

Benefits of volunteering: Starting a volunteer adventure after retirement has several advantages, including improved life, satisfaction, self-esteem, and overall well-being. Participating in worthwhile activities that benefit society might revive a feeling of purpose and nourish the spirit (MobileHelp, n.d.).

Getting started: Looking for volunteer activities that fit your interests and skills is a simple way to start your path of giving back. Matching retirees' interests with the community's needs may provide a rewarding volunteer experience (Indeed, n.d.).

Diverse volunteering paths: There are many ways to volunteer and improve the community, ranging from conventional positions to creative projects. By straying from the norm, retirees may discover new opportunities for service, which enhances their retirement and fosters mental health (Walden University, n.d.).

Managing one's mental health in retirement calls for a comprehensive strategy that accepts chances for development and satisfaction while acknowledging the difficulties. If retirees feed their souls with meaningful work and volunteerism, they may face the challenges of retirement with resiliency and purpose.

Soothing Mindfulness Practices: Nurturing Tranquility in Retirement
Although retirement offers many chances for introspection and personal development, it may also be stressful and anxious. Developing effective mindfulness practices is essential to supporting mental well-being during this transitional stage.

- **Breathing techniques for stress and anxiety:** Retirement is a pendulum that often swings with the weight of stress and worry. Using simple but effective breathing exercises provides calm in the middle of the chaos.
- **Abdominal breathing:** Intentional, deep breaths that activate the diaphragm are the basis of abdominal breathing, an essential technique in stress reduction. According to Verywell Mind, this

technique acts as a stabilizing influence, releasing stress and fostering serenity. **WebMD's stress-reduction methods:** A wide range of breathing exercises for stress management are available on WebMD. These breathing techniques, which range from diaphragmatic to roll breathing, work as a salve to calm the mind and relieve tension (WebMD).

- **Meditation techniques:** Within the practice of meditation, something significant happens. Retirement is an ideal opportunity to delve further into the broad field of meditation, using methods designed to promote calmness and inner peace.

- **HelpGuide's relaxation techniques:** HelpGuide offers an introduction to a variety of relaxation methods, including meditation. These techniques transcend the limitations of stress and bring peace via gradual muscular relaxation and guided imagery (HelpGuide, n.d.).

- **Meditation for depression:** Health.com explores the benefits of meditation for depression, showing how mindfulness may be a valuable tool for negotiating the emotional complexities of retirement (Health.com). **Positive psychology's meditation exercises:** Positive Psychology allows retirees to embark on a path of self-discovery through various meditation techniques, ranging from body scans to loving-kindness meditations. These techniques cultivate attention and enhance the mental landscape of retirees (Positive Psychology).

Adopting these mindfulness techniques becomes a harmonious tune in the retirement symphony, when stress and worry may generate dissonant notes. Every deliberate breath and mindful moment paints a picture of calm, creating a retirement full of inner serenity and well-being.

Welcome to "Entering Your Retirement Renaissance" in Chapter Eight. As our journey progresses, we welcome a time of rejuvenation, creativity, and self-discovery. Prepare to embrace the art of reinvention, discover new hobbies, and stoke your passions. Come along with us as we begin this exciting new chapter in your retirement journey, where inspiration and progress await you daily.

ENTERING YOUR RETIREMENT RENAISSANCE

" *"Live as if you were to die tomorrow. Learn as if you were to live forever."*

— *MAHATMA GANDHI*

WHY YOU SHOULD NEVER RETIRE FROM LEARNING: THE LIFELONG PURSUIT OF KNOWLEDGE

Continuing lifelong learning into retirement: Anglicare emphasizes the importance of lifelong learning, saying that acquiring knowledge enriches life at any age. Learning keeps the mind sharp, gives a sense of purpose, and helps connect with others, making retirement more fulfilling.

Retiring? Great! But don't stop learning: MarketWatch agrees that retirement opens up new opportunities for intellectual growth and exploration. Learning not only broadens horizons but also keeps the mind healthy and engaged in the retirement years.

The never-ending journey of learning: Terra Movement believes learning is a lifelong journey. It's about gaining facts and staying curious, adaptable, and open to change. Continuous learning keeps the spirit young and sparks a passion for discovery.

Benefits of senior education: Absolute Companion highlights the practical benefits of senior education, such as boosting self-esteem, improving cognitive function, and creating new social opportunities. Learning becomes a catalyst for a vibrant and purposeful retirement.

In alignment with these insights, Forbes emphasizes why successful people never stop learning. It's about staying relevant and gaining an advantage in innovation, resilience, and competitiveness.

As Inc. depicts learning is a continuous journey. The most successful individuals understand that knowledge is power and that pursuing learning leads to personal and professional growth.

In the dynamic world of retirement, where new possibilities await, embracing lifelong learning becomes a crucial choice. It's not just about acquiring information but committing to a life filled with curiosity, growth, and the sheer joy of discovery.

Avenues for Lifelong Learning - Unleashing the Curious Spirit of Retirement

Retirement is not the end but the beginning of a lifelong adventure of learning and exploration. Embracing knowledge in various forms can add vibrancy, purpose, and intellectual fulfillment to the golden years. Here's a guide to the many avenues for lifelong learning—tailored to the diverse preferences of retirees.

- **Learning opportunities for older adults and retirees:** Right at Home highlights numerous opportunities for lifelong learning specifically designed for older adults and retirees. From community classes to online platforms, there are several options to cater to different interests and preferences.

- **Formal Education: Pursuing Degrees and Certifications:** For those interested in traditional education, several colleges offer affordable or even free tuition for seniors. Kiplinger provides a comprehensive list covering all 50 states, ensuring accessibility and affordability. Money Talks News (n.d.) and AARP (n.d.) contribute to this list, providing valuable insights into institutions offering senior discounts and free classes.

- **Online college courses for seniors**: The digital age has revolutionized learning, with online classes allowing seniors to pursue degrees from their homes. Accredited institutions offer virtual courses, and guides like College Cliffs, and Online Colleges offer information on the best online degrees for seniors.

- **Instructions on studying for free as a senior**: To study for free as a senior, prospective learners can explore options like auditing classes without earning credits, taking advantage of senior discounts, or seeking out scholarship opportunities. Many universities provide accessible resources and opportunities for seniors to continue their education without financial burden. • As you embark on the exciting journey of lifelong learning, remember that curiosity knows no age. There are diverse avenues and endless opportunities to acquire knowledge and experience the joy of learning.

- **Informal learning - Unleashing your inner scholar after retirement:** Retirement is not about slowing down; it's an opportunity to explore, engage, and keep learning in new and exciting ways. Informal learning offers countless possibilities for seniors to stimulate their minds, develop new skills, and foster personal growth. Let's delve into the world of lifelong learning, where workshops, seminars, online courses, and language learning become the passport to an intellectually vibrant retirement.

- **Fun classes for seniors - What to look for and where to find them:** Seniors can embark on a journey of discovery by exploring a variety of fun and engaging classes. Many options are available, from arts and crafts to fitness and technology. Senior Services of America, Senior Lifestyle, Step2Health,

LoveToKnow, and ACTS Retirement provide comprehensive guides to finding classes tailored to the interests of older adults.

- **Switching to semi-retirement - Navigating the evolving landscape:** Retirement is evolving, and many retirees find themselves drawn to a semi-retired lifestyle, seeking parttime employment or exploring new careers. Understanding this changing landscape is crucial for those considering a change. Resources like A Wealth of Common Sense, Career Contacts, and Gottfried Somberg highlight the challenges and opportunities in this new retirement era, urging individuals to adapt and prepare for the changing dynamics.

- **Encore careers and second acts:** For those contemplating a second act in their careers, Investopedia, CNBC, Kiplinger, LinkedIn, Chateau La Jolla Inn, and Barefoot Consultants offer valuable insights into encore careers. These articles provide advice on financial considerations, self-assessment, and embracing the idea of a fulfilling second act in the professional realm.

As you venture into the world of informal learning and consider the evolving nature of retirement, remember that these are exciting chapters waiting to be written. Whether discovering new hobbies or redefining your professional journey, retirement is an opportunity to explore and embrace a life rich in knowledge and fulfillment.

BEST PART-TIME JOBS FOR RETIREES

Retirement doesn't have to mean the end of a fulfilling and engaging career. Part-time jobs for retirees offer opportunities to stay active, earn extra income, and explore new passions. Let's examine a curated list of resources highlighting the best part-time jobs for retirees to help them make a smooth transition into this inspiring time of life.

A curated list of part-time jobs for retirees: AARP's comprehensive guide provides insights into various part-time job options tailored for retirees, ensuring a seamless transition into the workforce. Indeed, it offers a valuable resource outlining the best jobs after retirement, considering flexibility, job satisfaction, and skill alignment. Bankrate provides a detailed overview of part-time jobs suitable for retirees, emphasizing financial considerations and work-life balance. U.S. News & World Report shares insights into fun and fulfilling part-time roles that pay well and bring joy. NewRetirement offers a diverse list of part-time jobs catering to retirees, providing options suitable for different preferences and skill sets.

Leaving your legacy - Mentoring and beyond: Retirement presents the opportunity to leave a lasting legacy by imparting knowledge and wisdom to others. Engaging in mentoring relationships and exploring creative outlets like writing are powerful ways to contribute to the community and share valuable experiences.

The joy of teaching and mentoring others: TIFWE explores five meaningful ways retirees can leave a legacy through mentoring, emphasizing the profound impact of guiding others. The U.S. Dream Academy and WITS Chicago highlight the joy of mentoring and why retirees make valuable mentors for youth. Enterprise Alumni discusses the benefits of alum mentor programs, showcasing the optimistic influence retirees can have on the professional development of others.

How to Be a Retiree Mentor + Tips: LinkedIn offers insights into becoming a mentor in retirement, guiding, and leveraging skills and experiences to benefit others. Demers Financial and Pantheon Wealth Planning share tips on being an effective mentor in retirement, emphasizing the reciprocal nature of mentorship.

Sharing Wisdom: Writing and Publishing in Retirement

Signs you should consider writing after retirement: Writing and Wellness provides a checklist of signs indicating that writing may be the perfect pursuit for retirees looking to share their stories. Jeanette LeBlanc and Hongkiat explore the signs suggesting you are a writer at heart, encouraging those considering writing after retirement.

Embarking on a post-retirement career, engaging in mentorship, or pursuing creative endeavors like writing can transform retirement into a vibrant and purposeful journey. By exploring these opportunities, retirees can continue contributing, learning, and finding joy in the next chapter of their lives.

Sharing your stories after retirement - A guide to publishing your writing: Retirement is a time of boundless possibilities, and one exciting avenue to explore is writing and publishing your own book. It may seem overwhelming initially, but with the proper guidance, it becomes a thrilling journey of self-expression and contribution. Let's discover the steps to writing and selfpublishing your book with valuable tips from experienced authors.

How to write and self-publish your book: Embarking on the journey of writing and self-publishing can be truly fulfilling. Here's a step-by-step guide to help you navigate the process:

Start with a vision: Clarify your vision before putting pen to paper. Retirement offers a unique perspective, and your book can capture a lifetime of experiences, wisdom, or newfound passions.

The three phases: Understand the three phases of writing and publishing your book: planning, writing, and marketing. Each phase is crucial for a successful self-publishing journey.

Utilize writing resources: To enhance your skills, take advantage of writing tips from seasoned authors. Insights from 150 writers and essential tips for authors can provide valuable guidance.

Writing tips for a successful book: Writing is an art, and honing your skills can significantly impact the quality of your book. Consider the following suggestions:

Inspiration from fellow writers: Gain inspiration from successful authors who share their advice based on years of experience.

Essential tips for authors: IngramSpark offers seven essential writing tips, covering aspects like character development, plot structure, and creating engaging narratives.

Comprehensive author's guide: NY Book Editors provides an extensive guide with 100 tips to help you become a better author, covering various aspects of the writing process.

Navigating the self-publishing process: Self-publishing is a dynamic process, and understanding the key steps is crucial for success:

Practical Guidance: Reedsy offers practical advice on self publishing, covering aspects like manuscript editing, book cover design, and marketing strategies.

Ingramspark's Guide: IngramSpark provides a comprehensive guide on self-publishing a book, offering insights into formatting, distribution, and reaching a broader audience.

AIA Academy: Publishing.com's AIA Academy is an online self publishing course that offers support, coaching, and artificial intelligence software for both beginners and advanced publishers.

Jane Friedman's Insights: Jane Friedman's blog delves into the intricacies of self-publishing, providing valuable insights and actionable steps for aspiring authors.

By combining your unique perspective with guidance from experienced authors, you can embark on a fulfilling writing and self publishing journey in retirement. Share your stories, wisdom, and passions with the world, leaving a lasting legacy that extends beyond your retirement years.

KEEPING THE GAME ALIVE

Now you have everything you need to successfully retire, it's time to pass on your newfound knowledge and show other readers where they can find the same help.

Simply by leaving your honest opinion of this book on Amazon, you will show other retirees where they can find the information they're looking for and inspire their passion for retirement.

Thank you for your help. The enthusiasm for retirement is shared when we pass on our knowledge – and you're helping me to do just that.

Scan the QR code below to leave your review:

CONCLUSION

I am pleased to see you get here after reading *Retirement Beyond Finances: Fulfilling Your Time with Purpose, Achieving a Healthier and Active Lifestyle, Creating Social Connections, and Embracing a New Way of Life.* This is a remarkable accomplishment, and I am honored you took the time to read my book. I hope you gained new insight and motivation into planning and enjoying your retirement journey. Let's take a moment to review the information we have covered:

- **The ABCs of Retirement**: Retirement is more than a phase; it's a whole alphabet of possibilities. Here are some of the things you should know about retirement. The ABCs include activities such as financial planning, the pursuit of hobbies, and cultivating well-being. The letter "A" stands for evaluating finances, while the letter "Z" stands for zeal in pursuing passions. To access the whole spectrum of options that retirement has to offer, you should investigate each letter.
- **Stepping into the Next Chapter - embracing a New Beginning**: The transition into retirement is analogous to flipping a page in the book of life. In the process of adopting this new chapter with excitement, you will leave behind the challenges of your previous job and enter a world where each day is a chance for personal development, exploration, and happiness. Seize the opportunity to rethink who you are and what you want to accomplish.

- **The "I" and "Me" in Retirement**: Retirement is a very personal experience. It is time to put the "I" and "Me" parts of life at the forefront of your priorities. Take some time to think about your requirements, goals, and objectives. For a satisfying retirement, it is essential to appreciate the significance of these personal aspects, whether it be the pursuit of long-forgotten interests or the use of time for self-care.

- **Finding Your Forever Home**: Retirement often provokes introspection over the perfect living arrangement for oneself. Whether you want to downsize to a tiny apartment, relocate to a busy neighborhood, or embrace the peacefulness of a rural location, choosing where to live for the rest of your life, or even for a season, is an important one. When designing a living environment conducive to your retirement aspirations, it is essential to consider your lifestyle, tastes, and long-term objectives. • **Retire, Roam, Rediscover, Repeat!** After reaching retirement age, one has the chance to travel the globe, one journey at a time. Roaming is not only a state of mind but also a way of thinking that involves ongoing discovery. The path through retirement is a never-ending cycle of discovery and exploration of oneself, whether it is via international travel, experiences in one's community, or just the pursuit of new interests.

  - **Retiring Strong:** Your physical health is the foundation of a happy and fulfilling retirement. Adopt a physically active lifestyle, prioritize regular exercise, and make preventative healthcare a primary issue. Retirement is a time to rejuvenate the body and ensure that each day is enjoyed to the maximum extent.

  - **Mental Wealth:** Cultivating a sound mind to provide a joyful retirement. Mental health is one of the most essential factors in a good retirement. Activities that engage the intellect, develop social relationships, and offer pleasure are all examples of activities that may help you cultivate a healthy mind. To make your mental health a priority, you should investigate various mindfulness techniques, participate in creative activities, and establish a support network. The key to a successful retirement is having a mind that can bounce back

from adversity. • **Entering Your Retirement Renaissance**:
Retirement is not a destination; instead, it is a renaissance. The eighth
and last phase in the retirement process. This phenomenon includes
the reawakening of dormant passions, the exploration of unexplored
territory, and the fulfillment of personal development. During this
period, you will have the opportunity to create your renaissance,
which will be filled with the colors of happiness, purpose, and
satisfaction.

THE INCREDIBLE JOURNEY OF KFC'S FOUNDER

Felloni (2015) shared on Business Insider that when Colonel Sanders was 65,
he embarked on a path that forever changed the fast-food world. Despite
facing challenges and starting from humble roots, the Colonel's recipe for
success was genuinely unique.

From cooking chicken at a service station to introducing the world to the
legendary Kentucky Fried Chicken, his story inspires us with resilience,
innovation, and a pursuit of culinary excellence. Born in 1890 on an Indiana
farm, Harland Sanders had to care for his siblings early in life. Dropping out
of school in 7th grade, he took on various jobs, served in the army, and started
his own business.

However, when he acquired a service station in Kentucky in 1930, Sanders'
true culinary adventure began. Using a pressure cooker to fry his chicken with
"11 herbs and spices," Sanders turned his modest eatery into a famous spot for
delicious meals. As word of his tasty chicken spread, so did his business
empire. Appointed as a Colonel by the Kentucky governor, Sanders became a
key figure in popular culture with his iconic white suit and tie.

Despite initial setbacks and losing his beloved restaurant, Sanders never
slowed down in retirement. With his secret recipe and unwavering

determination, he traveled across the country, making deals with restaurant owners to spread the joy of Kentucky Fried Chicken.

By 1965, Sanders had sold his franchise rights for an astounding $2 million, paving the way for KFC's worldwide success. Beyond money, Sanders' legacy is about sharing his love for food with the world, one bucket at a time. As we enjoy the Colonel's culinary creations, let's also cherish the lessons of persistence, passion, and striving for greatness that his life exemplifies.

From a Retired Banker to a Millionaire Freelancer

Once upon a time, a man named Jones Stacks lived in the bustling city of Rio de Janeiro. Jones had dedicated his life to the banking industry for years, climbing the corporate ladder and earning numerous accolades for his exceptional work. However, as he approached the age of 50, Jones realized that his health was deteriorating, and it was time to prioritize his well-being over his career.

With a heavy heart, Jones bid farewell to his illustrious banking career and embarked on a journey of retirement. However, life after retirement was less glamorous than he had envisioned. Health issues and mounting expenses made it challenging to make ends meet. But Jones was not one to give up easily. After recovering from his health concerns, he decided to explore new avenues to supplement his income and lead a fulfilling life in retirement.

Jones discovered the world of freelance writing during this quest for a new purpose. Despite having no prior experience in the field, Jones was determined to give it his all. He honed his writing skills, attended workshops, and immersed himself in the art of storytelling. His perseverance paid off when he landed a coveted spot on Urban Writers, a renowned freelancer platform.

With each passing day, Jones's confidence and expertise grew. He poured his heart and soul into every piece he crafted, earning accolades and recognition from clients and peers alike. What started as a means to make ends meet soon blossomed into a flourishing career. Today, Jones Stacks is not just a retired banker; he's a millionaire freelancer, earning five times more than he ever did in the banking industry.

Jones's story is a testament to the power of resilience, determination, and embracing change. His journey from retirement to freelancing success serves as a reminder that it's never too late to pursue your passions, reinvent yourself, and achieve greatness in unexpected ways. As Jones often says, "Retirement is not the end; it's a new beginning filled with endless possibilities."

A Wealth of Retiree Information in the Palm of Your Hands

The time has come for you to use all of your extensive expertise. There are many options and limitless potential. By incorporating this relevant information acquired into your remarkable new life, you can unleash development, spur innovation, and establish yourself as a visionary retiree, teaching and mentoring others in your golden years within these ever-growing business environments.

From Me to You

I urge you to use your newly acquired knowledge as you go on this thrilling adventure and to spread the word about this priceless resource to those in your sphere of influence. Not only may these suggestions alter your life, but they could also profoundly influence the lives of others.

Please consider sharing your opinions with the world if this book has helped you on your journey to becoming an exceptional retiree. Your Amazon or other bookshop review may act as a beacon, pointing a world of retirees toward their new beginnings and fulfillment in their retirement adventure.

Congratulations on reaching the end of this book. I hope it was an enjoyable read and that the information contained herein is invaluable to you in the coming days of your journey.

To your achievements, your infinite potential, in an era of unbounded possibilities.

Warm regards,

V. Spring

REFERENCES

A Place for Mom. (2021). *5 ways to keep your mind sharp.* https://www.aplaceformom.com/caregiver-resources/articles/sharp-mind

AARP. 2020.). *Free college classes.* https://www.aarp.org/work/careers/freecollege-classes/

Absolute Companion. (n.d.). *Benefits of senior education.* https://absolutecompanion.com/benefits-of-senior-education/

Adviser Investments. (2022). *Setting goals after retirement.* https://www.adviserinvestments.com/retirement/health-care/setting-goals-after-retirement/

Aged Care Guide. (n.d.). *Packing checklist for older people.* https://www.agedcareguide.com.au/information/packing-checklist-for-older-people Anglicare. (2023). *Why it's important you continue lifelong learning into retirement.* https://www.anglicare.org.au/media-centre/blog/why-its-important-youcontinue-lifelong-learning-into retirement/#:~:text=Continuing%20lifelong%20learning%20into%20your,whether%20at%2020%20or%2080.

Annie Anywhere. (n.d.). *How to plan a trip in 10 easy steps.* https://www.annieanywhere.com/how-to-plan-a-trip-in-10-easy-steps/

Annuity.org. (n.d.). *Retirement risks.* https://www.annuity.org/retirement/risks/

Arbor Company. (n.d.). *Top 10 exercises for seniors in retirement.* https://www.arborcompany.com/blog/top-10-exercises-for-seniors-in-retirement

AskChapter. (2023). *Senior hobbies for older men and women.* https://askchapter.org/ magazine/happy-retirement-tips/retirement-activities/senior-hobbies-forolder-men-and-women

Aspen Wealth Management. (n.d.). *Debunking 7 common retirement myths.* https://www.aspenwealthmgmt.com/resource-center/retirement/debunking-7common-retirement-myths/

Assisting Hands. (n.d.). *How to promote good heart health while aging.* https://www.assistinghands-il-wi.com/blog/how-to-promote-good-heart-health-whileaging/

Assisting Hands. (n.d.). *How to promote good heart health while aging.* https://www.assistinghands-il-wi.com/blog/how-to-promote-good-heart-health-whileaging/

AssureShift. (n.d.). *Pros and cons of relocating after retirement.* https://www.assureshift.in/blog/pros-and-cons-relocating-after-retirement

Avail. (n.d.). *Setting your retirement goals.* https://avail.app/public/articles/settingyour-retirement-goals

Aviva. (n.d.). *Mental health in retirement.* https://www.aviva.co.uk/retirement/health-wellbeing/mental-health-in-retirement/

Balance Pro. (n.d.). *10 tips for financial security after you retire.* https://www.balancepro.org/resources/articles/10-tips-for-financial-security-after-you-retire/

Battuta, I. (n.d.). *Traveling - it leaves you speechless, then turns you into a storyteller.* Goodreads. https://www.goodreads.com/quotes/508820-traveling-it-leavesyou-speechless-then-turns-you-into-a-storyteller

BBC Good Food. (n.d.). *10 foods to boost your brainpower.* https://www.bbcgoodfood.com/howto/guide/10-foods-boost-your-brainpower

Best Colleges. (n.d.). *Free college tuition for senior citizens.* https://www.bestcolleges.com/blog/free-college-tuition-senior-citizens/

Better Health Channel. (n.d.). *Nutrition needs when you're over 65.* https://www.betterhealth.vic.gov.au/health/healthyliving/Nutrition-needs-when-youreover-65

Better Health Channel. (n.d.). *Travel tips for seniors.* https://www.betterhealth.vic.gov.au/health/healthyliving/travel-tips-for-seniors

Better

Way In Home Care. (n.d.). *How to find passions in retirement.* https://abetterwayinhomecare.com/how-find-passions-retirement.html

Better5. (n.d.). *How to start a fitness routine after retirement: a guide for seniors.* https:// better5.com/how-to-start-a-fitness-routine-after-retirement-a-guide-forseniors/

Blakeford. (n.d.). *Top 14 travel tips for seniors: complete travel guide.* https://blakeford.com/top-14-travel-tips-for-seniors-complete-travel-guide/ BrainFacts.org.

(n.d.). *How the brain changes with age.* https://www.brainfacts.org/thinking-sens ing-and-behaving/aging/2019/how-the-brain-changes-with-age-083019

Brett Stumm. (n.d.). *Unusual hobbies for seniors.* https://brettstumm.com/unusualhobbies-for-seniors/

Brightland Homes. (n.d.). *Reasons to upsize home.* https://www.brightlandhomes.com/blog/reasons-to-upsize-home

Brown, L. (n.d.). *You are never too old to set another goal or to dream a new dream.* BrainyQuote. https://www.brainyquote.com/quotes/les_brown_119176

Business Insider. (n.d.). *Top ten countries for a comfortable retirement.* https://www.businessinsider.com/top-ten-countries-for-a-comfortable-retirement-2023-9

Canada Food Guide. (n.d.). *Tips for healthy eating: seniors.* https://food-guide.canada.ca/en/tips-for-healthy-eating/seniors/

Capital One. (n.d.). *Budget travel tips.* https://www.capitalone.com/learn-grow/more-than-money/budget-travel-tips/

Career Contacts. (n.d.). *The evolution of retirement: preparing for a new era.* https://www.careercontacts.ca/the-evolution-of-retirement-preparing-for-a-newera/

Cheapism. (n.d.). *Best travel destinations for seniors.* https://blog.cheapism.com/besttravel-destinations-for-seniors-15235/ CheapOair. (n.d.). Essential *hacks for senior citizens who love to travel.* https://www.cheapoair.com/miles-away/essential-hacks-for-senior-citizens-who-love-to-travel/

CHIP Reverse Mortgage. (n.d.). *Ways to improve heart health.* https://www.chip.ca/reverse-mortgage-resources/lifestyle/ways-to-improve-heart-health/

CHIP Reverse Mortgage. (n.d.). *Ways to improve heart health.* https://www.chip.ca/reverse-mortgage-resources/lifestyle/ways-to-improve-heart-health/

Cleveland Clinic. (n.d.). *How to age better by eating more healthfully.* https://health.clevelandclinic.org/how-to-age-better-by-eating-more-healthfully/

Cleveland Clinic. (n.d.). *Mild cognitive impairment.* https://my.clevelandclinic.org/health/diseases/17990-mild-cognitive-impairment

CNBC. (n.d.). *Can you afford a second act after retirement?* https://www.cnbc.com/2022/10/15/can-you-afford-a-second-act-after-retirement-what-to-askyourself.html

Collington. (n.d.). *7 fun brain activities to keep your mind sharp.* https://blog.collington.kendal.org/blog/7-fun-brain-activities-to-keep-your-mind-sharp

Columbia University Mailman School of Public Health. (n.d.). *Changes that occur in the aging brain: what happens when we get older.* https://www.publichealth.columbia.edu/news/changes-occur-aging-brain-what-happens-when-we-getolder

Conway Medical Center. (n.d.). *5 powerful ways seniors can quickly improve heart health.* https://www.conwaymedicalcenter.com/news/5-powerful-waysseniors-can-quickly-improve-heart-health/

Coombes, J. (n.d.). *The ultimate packing checklist for seniors going on holiday.* Medium.https://medium.com/@jacquicoombe/the-ultimate-packing-check list-for-seniors-going-on-holiday-63c17ce56e7d Discovery. (n.d.). *Retirement risk.* https://www.discovery.co.za/investments/retirement-risk

Doing More Today. (n.d.). *Creating a roadmap for your retirement goals.* https://doing moretoday.com/creating-a-roadmap-for-your-retirement-goals/

Doran, G.T. (1981) There's a SMART Way to Write Management's Goals and Objectives. Journal of Management Review, 70, 35-36. https://community.mis.temple.edu/mis0855002fall2015/files/2015/10/S.M.A.R.T-Way-Management-Review.pdf

EatingWell. (n.d.). 7 sneaky signs you could have cognitive decline. https://www.
eatingwell.com/article/7903274/7-sneaky-signs-you-could-have-
cognitivedecline-according-to-experts/

Empty Whole. (n.d.). *Top 5 things to prioritize in life.* https://emptywhole.com/
blogs/empty-whole/top-5-things-to-prioritize-in-life-empty-whole

EnterpriseAlumni. (n.d.). *Alumni mentor program.* https://enterprisealumni.com/
blog/alumni-mentor-program

Everyday Health. (n.d.). *Ways travel is good for your mental health.*
https://www.every dayhealth.com/emotional-health/ways-travel-is-good-for-your-
mental-health/ Expat Explore. (n.d.). Travel
etiquette: golden rules to follow. https://expatexplore.com/blog/travel-
etiquettegolden-rules-to-follow/ Fidelity.

(n.d.). *Retirement and budgeting.* https://www.fidelity.com/viewpoints/retirement/
retirement-and-budgeting

Financial Mentor. (n.d.). *Retirement myths.* https://www.financialmentor.com/
retirement-planning/retirement-myths/18185

Flying Angels. (n.d.). *Airplane travel hacks for seniors.* https://www.flyingangels.
com/airplane-travel-hacks-for-seniors/

Foley,

P. (n.d.). Retirement is a blank sheet of paper. It is a chance to redesign *your life into
some thing new and different.* Goodreads. https://www.goodreads.com/
quotes/10087483-retirement-is-a-blank-sheet-of-paper-it-is-a

Forbes. (n.d.). *6 retirement secrets from successful retirees.* https://www.forbes.com/
sites/stevevernon/2020/12/22/6-retirement-secrets-from-
successfulretirees/?sh=35c9733b49d3

Forbes. (n.d.). *Best and worst destinations for senior travel.*
https://www.forbes.com/ sites/lealane/2023/06/30/best-and-worst-destinations-for-
senior-travelaccording-to-new-data/?sh=5199ed6b67b4 Forbes.

(n.d.). *Best exercises for seniors.* https://www.forbes.com/health/healthy-
aging/bestexercises-for-seniors/

Forbes. (n.d.). W*hy the most successful people never stop learning and why you
shouldn't either.* https://www.forbes.com/sites/piasilva/2020/11/11/why-the-
mostsuccessful-people-never-stop-learning-and-why-you-shouldn't-either/?
sh=11bb18f539d7

Fosdick, H. E. (n.d.). *Don't simply retire from something; have something to retire
to.*
BrainyQuote. https://www.brainyquote.com/quotes/
harry_emerson_fosdick_100810

Freedom Square. (n.d.). *Hobby ideas for seniors*. https://freedomsquarefl.com/blog/hobby-ideas-for-seniors/

Frommer's. (n.d.). *Best vacation ideas and destinations for seniors.* https://www.frommers.com/slideshows/848278-best-vacation-ideas-and-destinations-forseniors

Gide, A. (n.d.). Man cannot discover new oceans unless he has the courage to lose *sight of the shore.* BrainyQuote. https://www.brainyquote.com/quotes/andre_gide_120088

Global View Investment Advisors. (n.d.). *Navigating your transition to retirement.*https://globalviewinv.com/navigating-your-transition-toretirement/

GOBankingRates. (n.d.). *Ugly truths about retirement*. https://www.gobankingrates.com/retirement/planning/ugly-truths-about-retirement/

GoodRx. (n.d.). *Benefits of travel: vacation for good health.* https://www.goodrx.com/ health-topic/mental-health/benefits-of-travel-vacation-good-health

Gottfried & Somberg. (n.d.). *The evolution of retirement.* https://www.gottfriedsomberg.com/content/TheEvolutionofRetirement

Grand Oaks. (n.d.). *9 heart-healthy tips for seniors.* https://www.grandoaksdc.org/9heart-healthy-tips-for-seniors/

Great Eastern Life. (n.d.). *Five retirement myths set straight*. https://www.greateasternlife.com/my/en/personal-insurance/understand-insurance/how-to-startplanning/retirement-planning/five-retirement-myths-set-straight.html

Great Oak Advisors. (n.d.). *Four helpful tips to successfully move after retirement.* https://www.greatoakadvisors.com/four-helpful-tips-to-successfully-moveafter-retirement/

Great Senior Living. (n.d.). *Senior travel.* https://www.greatseniorliving.com/articles/senior-travel

Greater Alliance. (n.d.). *Protect your wealth: The importance of financial security.* https://www.greateralliance.org/protect-your-wealth-the-importance-of-finan cial-security/

Guide for Seniors. (n.d.). *Packing for a trip.* https://guideforseniors.com/seniortravel/travel-tips/packing-for-a-trip/

Harvard Health Publishing. (n.d.). *6 simple steps to keep your mind sharp at any Age.* https://www.health.harvard.edu/mind-and-mood/6-simple-steps-to-keepyour-mind-sharp-at-any-age

Harvard Health Publishing. (n.d.). *Foods linked to better brainpower.* https://www.health.harvard.edu/healthbeat/foods-linked-to-better-brainpower

Health in Aging. (n.d.). *Safe travel tips for older adults.* https://www.healthinaging.org/tools-and-tips/tip-sheet-safe-travel-tips-older-adults

Healthline. (n.d.). *11 best foods to boost your brain and memory.* https://www.health
line.com/nutrition/11-brain-foods

Healthline. (n.d.). *Brain exercises: mental health.* https://www.healthline.com/
health/mental-health/brain-exercises

Healthline. (n.d.). *Healthy eating for seniors.* https://www.healthline.com/health/
healthy-eating-for-seniors

Healthline. (n.d.). *Senior workouts: health benefits and sample routine.* https://www.
healthline.com/health/everyday-fitness/senior-workouts

HealthNews. (n.d.). *How having a hobby benefits your health.* https://healthnews.
com/family-health/healthy-living/how-having-a-hobby-benefits-your-health/

HelpGuide. (n.d.). *Adjusting to retirement.*https://www.helpguide.org/articles/ aging-
issues/adjusting-to-
retirement.htm#:~:text=You%20may%20grieve%20the%20loss,as%20clinical%
20depression%20or%20anxiety.

HelpGuide. (n.d.). *Adjusting to retirement.*https://www.helpguide.org/articles/ aging-
issues/adjusting-to-retirement.htm

HelpGuide. (n.d.). *Eating well as you age.*https://www.helpguide.org/articles/
healthy-eating/eating-well-as-you-age.htm

Henry Ford Health System. (n.d.). *8 ways to keep your mind sharp.* https://www.
henryford.com/blog/2016/06/8-ways-keep-mind-sharp

Here to Help. (n.d.). *Making a positive mental transition to retirement.* https://www.
heretohelp.bc.ca/making-positive-mental-transition-retirement

HeyMondo. (n.d.). *10 tips for traveling on a budget.*
https://heymondo.com/blog/10tips-travel-budget/

Holiday Retirement. (n.d.). *Creating the ultimate bucket list for seniors.*
https://www. holidayretirement.com/creating-the-ultimate-bucket-list-for-
seniors/

HonestMoney. (n.d.). *Five things I wish I knew before I retired.* https://honestmoney.
ca/stories/five-things-i-wish-i-knew-before-i-retired-1

Hongkiat. (n.d.). *Signs you are a writer.*https://www.hongkiat.com/blog/signs-
youare-a-writer/

HumanGood. (n.d.). *Breaking free from retirement myths.* https://www.humangood.
org/resources/senior-living-blog/breaking-free-from-retirement-myths

I'm Thinking of Retiring. (n.d.). *Unusual hobbies for seniors.* https://imthinkingofre
tiring.com/unusual-hobbies-for-seniors/

Inc.com. (n.d.). *4 reasons why we should never stop learning.*
https://www.inc.com/ajagrawal/4-reasons-why-we-should-never-stop-
learning.html

Indeed. (n.d.). *Goal-setting techniques.* https://www.indeed.com/career-advice/
career-development/goal-setting-techniques

Indeed. (n.d.). *Retirement goals.* https://www.indeed.com/career-
advice/careerdevelopment/retirement-goals

IngramSpark. (n.d.). *7 essential writing tips for authors.* https://www.ingramspark.
com/blog/7-essential-writing-tips-for-authors

IngramSpark. (n.d.). *How to self-publish a book.* https://www.ingramspark.com/
how-to-self-publish-a-book

Inspired by Insiders. (n.d*.). Retirement tips boomers wish they knew.* https://inspired
byinsiders.com/retirement-tips-boomers-wish-they-knew/

Inspired Villages. (n.d.). *How to create an exercise routine in retirement.*
https://www.
inspiredvillages.co.uk/blog/how-to-create-an-exercise-routine-in-retirement

Institute for Faith, Work & Economics. (n.d.). *5 ways to leave a legacy: mentoring in
retirement.* https://tifwe.org/5-ways-to-leave-a-legacy-mentoring-inretirement/

International Living. (n.d.). *The best places to retire.* https://internationalliving.com/
the-best-places-to-retire/

Investopedia. (n.d.). *10 secure retirement tips.* https://www.investopedia.com/arti
cles/retirement/06/10secureretirementtips.asp

Investopedia. (n.d.). *4 phases of retirement and how to budget them.* https://www.
investopedia.com/articles/personal-finance/110315/4-phases-retirementand-how-
budget-them.asp

Investopedia. (n.d.). *Encore career.*
https://www.investopedia.com/terms/e/encorecareer.asp

Investopedia. (n.d.). The 6 *stages of retirement.* https://www.investopedia.com/arti
cles/retirement/07/sixstages.asp

Jane Friedman. (n.d.). *Self-publish your book.* https://janefriedman.com/selfpublish-
your-book/

Jeanette   LeBlanc. (n.d.).   *Write   your
book.* https://www.jeanetteleblanc.com/ writeyourbook/

Katie Reed. (n.d.). *Self-care is giving the world the best of you, instead of what's left
of you.* [Quozio]. https://quozio.com/quote/127d9056/1025/selfcare-is-givingthe-
world-the-best-of-you-instead-of-what-s-left-of-you

Kiplinger. (n.d.). *Free or cheap college for retirees in all 50 states.* https://www.
kiplinger.com/slideshow/retirement/t065-s001-free-or-cheap-college-forretirees-
in-all-50-state/index.html

Kiplinger. (n.d.). *Second-act careers.* https://www.kiplinger.com/second-act-retire
ment-job

Kolluri, A., & Hutchins, D. (2017). *Life priorities: a new approach to retirement planning.* Pension Research Council. https://pensionresearchcouncil.wharton. upenn.edu/wp-content/uploads/2017/02/05-Kolluri-and-Hutchins.pdf Landmark Senior Living. (n.d.). *Preparing for a trip as a senior.* https://landmarkse niorliving.com/preparing-for-a-trip-as-a-senior/ Lee Health. (n.d.). *The mental health benefits of traveling.* https://www.leehealth.org/health-and-wellness/ healthy-news-blog/mental-health/the-mental-health-benefits-of-traveling

Life Care Services. (n.d.). *7 senior travel tips: what to consider when planning a trip.* https://www.lifecareservices.com/insights-for-senior-living/insights-detail/7senior-travel-tips-what-to-consider-when-planning-a-trip

LifeConnect 24. (n.d.). *Top 15 hobby ideas for older people.* https://www.lifeconnec t24.co.uk/blog/top-15-hobby-ideas-for-older-people/

Life Matters Financial Planning. (n.d.). *6 top tips to make a smooth transition* into retirement. https://lifemattersfp.com/6-top-tips-to-make-a-smooth-transi tion-into-retirement/

Lifehack. (n.d.). *List of priorities.* https://www.lifehack.org/876081/list-of-priorities

LinkedIn. (n.d.). *What's your second act: finding and embracing retirement.* https:// www.linkedin.com/pulse/whats-your-second-act-finding-embracing-retire ment-tammy-vigue

LinkedIn. (n.d.). *Why you should never stop learning: benefits of lifelong education.*https://www.linkedin.com/pulse/why-you-should-never-stop-learn ing-benefits-lifelong-education-kumar

Literary Hub. (n.d.). I Talked to 150 Writers and Here's the Best Advice They Had. https://lithub.com/i-talked-to-150-writers-and-heres-the-best-advice-theyhad/

Living Confidently. (n.d.). *What I wish I had known before retirement.* https://living confidently.com/what-i-wish-i-had-known-before-retirement/

Mahatma Gandhi. (n.d.). *Live as if you were to die tomorrow. Learn as if you were to live forever.* [BrainyQuote]. [https://www.brainyquote.com/quotes/ mahatma_gandhi_133995

MarketWatch. (n.d.). *Retiring great, but don't stop learning.* https://www.market watch.com/story/retiring-great-but-dont-stop-learning-11655418749

MassMutual. (n.d.). *Upsizing in retirement.* https://blog.massmutual.com/retiringinvesting/upsizing-in-retirement

Mayo Clinic. (n.d.). *Mild cognitive impairment: symptoms and causes.* https://www. mayoclinic.org/diseases-conditions/mild-cognitive-impairment/symptomscauses/syc-20354578

McLain Properties. (n.d.). *7 signs it's time to upsize.* https://www.mclainproperties. com/blog/7-signs-its-time-to-upsize

Medical News Today. (n.d.). *Foods that may help preserve your memory.* https://www. medicalnewstoday.com/articles/324044

Medical News Today. (n.d.). *What happens when we get older?* https://www.medical newstoday.com/articles/319185#Recent-discoveries-in-brain-aging

Mental Health Foundation. (n.d.). *How to look after your mental health in later life.* https://www.mentalhealth.org.uk/explore-mental-health/publications/howlook-after-your-mental-health-later-life

Merrill Lynch. (n.d.). *Big retirement risks and how to prepare for them.* https://www. ml.com/articles/big-retirement-risks-and-how-to-prepare-for-them.html

Money Talks News. (n.d.). *Colleges with senior discounts.* https://www.moneytalk snews.com/slideshows/colleges-with-senior-discounts/

MoneySmartGuides. (n.d.). 10 *hidden retirement challenges nobody talks about.* https://www.moneysmartguides.com/10-hidden-retirement-challengesnobody-talks-about

My Moving Reviews. (n.d.). *Pros and cons of moving after retirement.* https://www. mymovingreviews.com/move/pros-and-cons-of-moving-after-retirement/

My Relatives Care. (n.d.). *Heart health: easy checklist for seniors.* https://myrela tivescare.com/blog/heart-health-easy-checklist-seniors/

My Relatives Care. (n.d.). *Heart health: easy checklist for seniors.* https://myrela tivescare.com/blog/heart-health-easy-checklist-seniors/

National Center for Biotechnology Information. (n.d.). *The effects of aging on the brain.* https://www.ncbi.nlm.nih.gov/pmc/articles/ PMC2596698/#:~:text=The%20brain%20shrinks%20with%20increasing,levels %20of%20neurotransmitters%20and%20hormones

National Council on Aging. (n.d.). *Safe travel tips for older adults.* https://www.ncoa. org/article/safe-travel-tips-for-older-adults

National Institute on Aging. (n.d.). *Heart health and aging.* https://www.nia.nih.gov/ health/heart-health-and-aging

National Institute on Aging. (n.d.). *How older adults can get started with exercise.* https://www.nia.nih.gov/health/how-older-adults-can-get-started-exercise

National Institute on Aging. (n.d.). *How the aging brain affects thinking.* https:// www.nia.nih.gov/health/how-aging-brain-affects-thinking

NBC News. (n.d.). 5 *scientifically proven health benefits of traveling abroad.* https:// www.nbcnews.com/better/wellness/5-scientifically-proven-health-benefitstraveling-abroad-n759631 NCOA. (n.d.). Healthy eating *tips for seniors.* https://www.ncoa.org/article/healthy-eating-tips-for-seniors

Neel Raman. (n.d.). 5 *reasons why you need to have a bucket list.* https://neelraman. com/5-reasons-why-you-need-to-have-a-bucket-list/

NerdWallet. (n.d.). *How to safeguard your mental health in retirement.* https://www.nerdwallet.com/article/finance/mental-health-risks-retirement

New Retirement. (n.d.). *What to do in retirement.* https://www.newretirement.com/retirement/what-to-do-in-retirement/

NewRetirement. (n.d.). *Retirement surprises: what I wish I knew before I retired.* https://www.newretirement.com/retirement/retirement-surprises-what-iwish-i-knew-before-i-retired/

NewRetirement. (n.d.). *Transition to retirement: exceptional tips.* https://www.newretirement.com/retirement/transition-to-retirement-exceptional-tips/

Next Avenue. (n.d.). *Write a book.* https://www.nextavenue.org/write-a-book/

NI Direct. (n.d.). *Healthy eating for older adults.* https://www.nidirect.gov.uk/articles/healthy-eating-older-adults

NIH Federal Credit Union. (n.d.). *8 hard truths about retirement.* https://www.nihfcu.org/8-hard-truths-about-retirement/

Nomadic Matt. (n.d.). *Planning a trip.* https://www.nomadicmatt.com/travelblogs/planning-a-trip/

NY Book Editors. (n.d.). *100 tips to help you become a better author.* https://nybookeditors.com/2019/04/100-tips-to-help-you-become-a-better-author/

One891 Financial Life. (n.d.). *Setting retirement goals.* https://www.1891financiallife.com/setting-retirement-goals/

Online Colleges. (n.d.). *Online colleges for senior citizens.* https://www.onlinecolleges.net/resources/online-colleges-senior-citizens/

Practical Wanderlust. (n.d.). *How to plan a trip: travel planning tips.* https://practicalwanderlust.com/how-to-plan-a-trip-travel-planning-tips/

Psych Central. (n.d.). *Coping with retirement depression.* https://psychcentral.com/depression/retirement-depression

Quora. (n.d.). *What advice about retirement do you wish had been shared with you before retiring?* https://www.quora.com/What-advice-about-retirement-do-youwish-had-been-shared-with-you-before-retiring

Ramsey Solutions. (n.d.). *5 steps to planning a memorable vacation.* https://www.ramseysolutions.com/saving/5-steps-to-planning-memorable-vacation

Ramsey Solutions. (n.d.). *Achieving financial security.* https://www.ramseysolutions.com/budgeting/financial-security

Reader's Digest UK. (n.d.). *The health benefits of having a hobby.* https://www.readersdigest.co.uk/health/wellbeing/the-health-benefits-of-having-a-hobby

Reader's Digest. (n.d.). *Trips for seniors: the best vacation ideas.* https://www.rd.com/list/trips-for-seniors/

Reedsy. (n.d.). *How to write a book*. https://blog.reedsy.com/how-to-write-a-book/

Rest Less. (n.d.). *Ways to keep your mind sharp as you age.* https://restless.co.uk/health/healthy-mind/ways-to-keep-your-mind-sharp-as-you-age/

Retirely. (n.d.). *Bucket list for retirement*.https://retirely.co/bucket-list-retirement/

Retirement Stewardship. (n.d.). *You can self-publish a book.* https://retirementstewardship.com/2021/05/26/you-can-self-publish-a-book/

Retirement Tips and Tricks. (n.d.). *Best hobbies in retirement*. https://retirementtipsandtricks.com/best-hobbies-in-retirement/

Retirement Tips and Tricks. (n.d.). *How to get a retirement hobby*. https://retirementtipsandtricks.com/how-to-get-a-retirement-hobby/

Retirement Wisdom. (n.d.). *Leisure and social pursuits*. https://www.retirementwisdom.com/blogs/leisure-and-social/

RetireWell. (n.d.). *Budget planner*. https://www.retirewell.com.au/files/ budget_planner.pdf

Right at Home. (n.d.). *Lifelong learning opportunities for older adults and retirees*. https://www.rightathome.net/blog/lifelong-learning-opportunities-for-olderadults-and-retirees

Riviera Travel. (n.d.). *12 international etiquette tips every traveler should know*. https:// www.rivieratravel.co.uk/blog/12-international-etiquette-tips-every-travellershould-know

Road Scholar. (n.d.). Packing *tips.* https://www.roadscholar.org/senior-travel-tips/packing-tips/

Robert Schuller. (n.d.). *Tough times never last, but tough people do!*Goodreads]. [https://www.goodreads.com/en/book/show/1374307

Royal Moving Co. (n.d.). *Pros and cons of moving after retirement.* https://royalmovingco.com/blog/pros-and-cons-of-moving-after-retirement/

Sam Levenson. (n.d.). *As you grow older, you will discover that you have two hands, one for helping yourself, the other for helping others*. [Quote Fancy]. https://quotefancy. com/quote/2214307/Sam-Levenson-As-you-grow-older-you-will-discoverthat-you-have-two-hands-one-for-helping

Satori Wealth. (n.d.). *Relocating in retirement: Practical tips.* https://satoriwealth. com/relocating-in-retirement-practical-tips/

Savoteur. (n.d.). *11 travel hacks older travelers shared for travelers who are 50+.* https://savo teur.com/11-travel-hacks-older-travelers-shared-for-travelers-who-are-50/

Seasons Retirement Communities. (n.d.). *Transition to retirement.* https://seasonsretirement.com/transition-to-retirement/

Second Wind Movement. (n.d.). *Retirement goals.* https://secondwindmovement.com/retirement-goals/

Second wind movement. (n.d.). *Retirement stages.*
https://secondwindmovement.com/ retirement-stages/

Self-Publishing School. (n.d.). *How to publish a book.* https://self-publishingschool.
com/how-to-publish-a-book/

Senior Lifestyle. (n.d.). *7 best exercises for seniors (and a few to avoid).* https://www.
seniorlifestyle.com/resources/blog/7-best-exercises-for-seniors-and-a-fewto-avoid/

Senior Services of America. (n.d.). *12 heart-healthy activities for seniors.* https://
seniorservicesofamerica.com/blog/12-heart-healthy-activities-
forseniors/#:~:text=To%20help%20maintain%20heart%20health,avocados%2C
%20raw%20nuts%2C%20olive%20oil

Senior Services of America. (n.d.). *Great ideas for hobbies after retirement.* https://
seniorservicesofamerica.com/blog/great-ideas-for-hobbies-after-retirement/

Senior Travel Central. (n.d.). *15 best travel safety tips for seniors.*
https://www.senior travelcentral.com/15-best-travel-safety-tips-for-seniors.html

Share NZ. (n.d.). *How to navigate the transition to retirement.* https://sharenz.com/
how-to-navigate-the-transition-to-retirement/

Shyft Moving. (n.d.). *Moving after retirement.* https://www.shyftmoving.com/blog/
moving-after-retirement

SimOptions. (n.d.). *Travel etiquette
tips.*https://www.simoptions.com/traveletiquette-tips/

Sixty and Me. (n.d.). *20 serious and fun things you can do in retirement.* https://
sixtyandme.com/20-serious-and-fun-things-you-can-do-in-retirement/

Sixty and Me. (n.d.). *The 3 phases of writing and publishing your own book in
retirement.* https://sixtyandme.com/the-3-phases-of-writing-and-publishingyour-
own-book-in-retirement/

Small Business Trends. (n.d.). *Travel etiquette tips.* https://smallbiztrends.com/
2023/10/travel-etiquette-tips.html?expand_article=1

SmarterTravel. (n.d.). *7 safety tips for senior travelers.* https://www.smartertravel.
com/7-safety-tips-senior-travelers/

SoFi. (n.d.). *How to determine your retirement goals.* https://www.sofi.com/learn/
content/how-to-determine-your-retirement-goals/

Soni, M.K. (n.d.). *Retire from work, but not from life.* Quotery. https://www.quotery.
com/quotes/retire-work-not-life

Steinbeck, J. (n.d.). *People don't take trips, trips take people.* Goodreads.
https://www.
goodreads.com/quotes/1311410-people-don-t-take-trips-trips-take-people

Stumm, B. (n.d.). *Best us travel destinations for seniors.*
https://brettstumm.com/bestus-travel-destinations-for-seniors/

Terra Movement. (n.d.). *Never stop learning.*https://www.terramovement.com/never-stop-learning/

The Balance. (n.d.). *How to make a retirement budget.* https://www.thebalance.com/how-to-make-a-retirement-budget-2388345

The Early Airway. (n.d.). *Travel etiquette tips.* https://theearlyairway.com/traveletiquette-tips/#:~:text=Treat%20locals%20well%20and%20understand,tourists%20for%20years%20to%20come.

The Motley Fool. (2015, April 21). An audacious retirement goal: upsize your *home.* https://www.fool.com/retirement/general/2015/04/21/an-audaciousretirement-goal-upsize-your-home.aspx

The Motley Fool. (n.d.). *15 hard truths about retirement that you're not expecting.* https://www.fool.com/slideshow/15-hard-truths-about-retirement-thatyoure-not-expecting/?slide=2

The Motley Fool. (n.d.). *15 questions to ask before relocating in retirement.* https://www.fool.com/slideshow/15-questions-to-ask-before-relocating-in-retire ment/?slide=2

The Poor Traveler. (n.d.). *Senior citizen-friendly destinations.* https://www.thepoor traveler.net/2017/08/senior-citizen-friendly-destinations/

The Washington Post. (n.d.). *Understanding five common retirement risk factors.* https://www.washingtonpost.com/sf/brand-connect/wp/enterprise/wells-fargo/understanding-five-common-retirement-risk-factors/

TIAA. (n.d.). *Retirement expense-income worksheets.* https://www.tiaa.org/public/pdf/r/retirement_expense-income_worksheets.pdf

TowneBank. (n.d.). *Four tips for financial security.* https://www.townebank.com/personal/resource/retirement/savings/four/

Travel + Leisure. (n.d.). *Ways travel is good for your health.* https://www.trave landleisure.com/trip-ideas/yoga-wellness/ways-travel-is-good-for-yourhealth

Travelers Worldwide. (n.d.). *Science-Backed Health Benefits of Traveling.* Travelers

Triton Financial Group. (n.d.). *The crucial role of budgeting for retirement planning.* https://tritonfinancialgroup.com/the-crucial-role-of-budgeting-for-retire ment-planning/#:~:text=Budgeting%20serves%20as%20a%20compass,you'll%20need%20each%20year.

Tru Travels. (n.d.). *Travel etiquette.* https://www.trutravels.com/travel-etiquette U.S. Dream Academy. (n.d.). *Life lessons: retirees are valuable mentors for youth.* https://www.usdreamacademy.org/life-lessons-retirees-are-valuable-mentorsfor-youth

U.S. News & World Report. (n.d.). *8 tips for finding a hobby in retirement*.https:// money.usnews.com/money/blogs/on-retirement/articles/8-tips-for-findinga-hobby-in-retirement

U.S. News & World Report. (n.d.). *Steps to take before relocating in retirement*. https:// money.usnews.com/money/retirement/baby-boomers/articles/steps-to-takebefore-relocating-in-retirement

U.S. News & World Report. (n.d.). *Top travel destinations for retirees*. https://money. usnews.com/money/retirement/baby-boomers/slideshows/top-travel-destina tions-for-retirees

U.S. News. (n.d.). *Best countries to retire*. https://www.usnews.com/news/best-coun tries/best-countries-to-retire?slide=2

UnityPoint Health. (n.d.). *15 brain foods that may help preserve your memory*. https:// www.unitypoint.org/news-and-articles/15-brain-foods-that-may-helppreserve-your-memory

University of Oregon. (n.d.). *Retirement budget worksheet*. https://hr.uoregon.edu/ content/retirement-budget-worksheet

Utah State University Extension. (n.d.). *How hobbies improve mental health*. https:// extension.usu.edu/mentalhealth/articles/how-hobbies-improve-mental-health

Verywell Fit. (n.d.). *Exercise and activity plan for newly retired*. https://www.verywell fit.com/exercise-and-activity-plan-for-newly-retired-4120207

Verywell Mind. (n.d.). *Tips for adjusting to retirement*. https://www.verywellmind. com/tips-for-adjusting-to-retirement-4173709

Vigue, T. (n.d.). *How to find new hobbies and interests in retirement*. LinkedIn. https:// www.linkedin.com/pulse/how-find-new-hobbies-interests-retirementtammy-vigue

Waywiser. (n.d.). *8 best us vacation ideas for seniors*. https://waywiser.com/word tothewise/8-best-us-vacation-ideas-for-seniors/

We Are Global Travellers. (n.d.). *Tips for traveling on a budget*. https://weareglobal travellers.com/2020/05/tips-travelling-on-a-budget/

Wealth of Common Sense. (n.d.). *The evolution of retirement*. https://awealthofcom monsense.com/2023/08/the-evolution-of-retirement/

WebMD. (n.d.). *Health benefits of hobbies*.https://www.webmd.com/balance/healthbenefits-of-hobbies

Western & Southern Financial Group. (n.d.). *How to set retirement goals*. https:// www.westernsouthern.com/retirement/how-to-set-retirement-goals

Western & southern financial group. (n.d.). *Retirement myths*. https://www.western southern.com/retirement/retirement-myths#:,

Wildpine Residence. (n.d.). *Living retirement to its fullest: Tips for creating a bucket list*. https://wildpineresidence.ca/living-retirement-to-its-fullest-tips-for-creatinga-bucket-list/

Wildpine Residence. (n.d.). *The 5 stages of retirement everyone will go through*. https:// wildpineresidence.ca/the-5-stages-of-retirement-everyone-will-go-through/

WITS Chicago. (n.d.). *Benefits of mentoring for retired adults*. https://witschicago.org/benefits-of-mentoring-for-retired-adults

Writing & Wellness. (n.d.). *Is writing after retirement right for you?* https://writingandwellness.com/2021/04/14/is-writing-after-retirement-right-for-you/

Yahoo Finance. (n.d.). *5 uncomfortable truths about retirement*. https://finance.yahoo.com/news/5-uncomfortable-truths-retirement-really-110000039.html

www.ingramcontent.com/pod-product-compliance
Lightning Source LLC
Chambersburg PA
CBHW021226130626
46554CB00004B/1390